Werner Blaser

Tomsk

Texture in Wood – Texture en Bois – Textur in Holz

Birkhäuser Verlag
Basel · Boston · Berlin

Traduction française: Danièle Renard

Translation of German texts into English: R.H. Williamson

Übersetzung des russischen Textes ins Deutsche: Mara Dollinger

A CIP catalogue record for this book is available from the Library of Congress, Washington D.C., USA.

Die Deutsche Bibliothek – CIP-Einheitsaufnahme

Tomsk : Textur in Holz / Werner Blaser. [Trad. française: Danièle Renard.
Transl. of German texts into English: R.H. Williamson]. –
Basel ; Boston ; Berlin : Birkhäuser, 1994
  ISBN 3-7643-2849-5
NE: Blaser, Werner; Renard, Danièle [Übers.]

© 1994 Birkhäuser Verlag, Postfach 133, CH-4010 Basel, Schweiz
Printed on acid-free paper produced of chlorine-free pulp
Cover design and all photographs by the author
ISBN 3-7643-2849-5
ISBN 0-8176-2849-5

9 8 7 6 5 4 3 2 1

Contents
Sommaire
Inhalt

From the earliest times, people have created dwellings – a visible sign of every popular culture. In architecture, from the historical viewpoint, wood is the most primary of materials. Wood is always available, yet at the same time it demands a thorough knowledge of its properties and possibilities. Craftsmen have complied with these characteristics in order to enter into a true dialogue with their material. It is almost impossible to escape the magic of wood and not to be charmed by the warmth which it emanates.

The houses of Tomsk are testimonies to the closeness of the relationship between man and wood. The harsh climate, the monotonous landscape and the isolated position of the town at first produced dwellings whose sole purpose was to ensure survival. The necessary building materials were there in the form of spruce, pine and larch. The technique was already known: round log construction with corner halvings.

Later came easier and more cheerful times – times when life could be enjoyed. The dark huts of the pioneers were succeeded by friendly facades. More light entered the rooms, and the creativity of the craftsmen was awakened.

The streets became, in effect, a gallery in which the pictures were the houses themselves with their windows and surrounds, ornamented cornices, carved bargeboards and in some cases wood claddings over the log construction. The character of the facades is determined by the window openings, which, as vertical components, combine with the horizontals of the log structure as cardinal elements in the architectural composition. The decor, although it often seems over-lavish, counterbalances the greyness of the winter days and helps to make them more bearable.

Tomsk is an example of collective design and the creation of architectural works by a community. Within this collective, each house speaks a message of its own which is still understood today: It is a spontaneous expression of the quest for happiness.

Werner Blaser tirelessly devotes himself to a worldwide search for the relationships between material and structure. With this book, he again makes us eye-witnesses to his achievement.

Préface

Le cadre de vie de l'homme est, depuis l'aube des temps, la représentation la plus tangible de la culture d'un peuple. Dans l'histoire, le bois est le premier matériau de l'architecture. S'il est pleinement disponible, en retour, il réclame une parfaite connaissance de ses possibilités et de ses exigences et incite les maîtres d'œuvre à acquérir une discipline qui les conduit à dialoguer avec lui. Il est alors difficile de se soustraire à son attrait, à son charme, et à la chaleur de sa présence.

Les maisons de Tomsk témoignent de cette complicité entre l'homme et le bois. La rudesse du climat, le paysage plat, très uniforme, voire monotone, joints à l'isolement de la ville, ont incité à créer, dans un premier temps, des lieux pour survivre. Le matériau est présent: pin, épicéa, mélèze. La technique est connue: rondins avec assemblages à mi-bois.

Vient ensuite le temps de vivre, de la gaieté, de la joie. A l'austère abri des fondateurs succède le sourire des façades. La lumière pénètre dans les demeures et cet événement libère la créativité de l'artisan.

Les rues deviennent galeries où apparaissent les tableaux, les baies, les encadrements, les rives animées, les couronnements sculptés et, pour partie, l'habillage des parois en rondins. Les façades sont parées d'une vêture en clins ouvragés qui respecte l'ordonnancement majeur de cette architecture: l'horizontalité pour l'enceinte, la verticalité pour les ouvertures. Le décor est parfois chargé mais il doit rester lisible dans la longue grisaille de l'hiver.

Tomsk est un exemple de ces œuvres collectives où chacun apporte un message qui vient aujourd'hui jusqu'à nous: c'est l'expression spontanée d'une population en quête de bonheur.

Il appartenait à Werner Blaser, inlassable chercheur de matériaux et de structures à travers le monde, de nous faire partager ce témoignage.

Geleitwort

Seit Urzeiten haben sich Menschen Behausungen geschaffen – ein sichtbares Zeichen jeder Volkskultur. In der Architektur ist, geschichtlich betrachtet, das Holz das ursprünglichste Material. Holz ist stetig verfügbar; gleichzeitig verlangt es genaue Kenntnisse seiner Eigenschaften und Möglichkeiten. Diesen Eigenheiten haben sich die Handwerker unterworfen, um mit dem Material förmlich einen Dialog zu führen. Es ist kaum möglich, sich diesem Zauber des Holzes zu entziehen, seinem Charme und seiner warmen Ausstrahlung.

Die Häuser von Tomsk sind Zeugen dieser Verbundenheit zwischen Mensch und Holz. Das harte Klima, die gleichförmige und monoton wirkende Landschaft sowie die isolierte Lage dieser Stadt haben ursprünglich Behausungen allein zum Überleben verlangt. Die Baumaterialien dazu waren vorhanden: Fichten, Kiefern und Lärchen. Die Technik war bekannt: Blockbau aus Rundholz mit Eckverblattungen.

Später kamen bessere und frohe Zeiten – Zeiten zum Leben. Auf die dunklen Hütten der Gründer folgten freundliche Fassaden. Die Räume erhielten mehr Licht, und die Kreativität der Handwerker wurde geweckt.

Die Straßen wurden förmlich zur Galerie – die Häuser waren die Bilder: mit ihren Fenstern, den Umrahmungen, den verzierten Gesimsen, den geschnitzten Dachabschlüssen und zeitweilig auch mit verkleideten Blockbaufassaden. Die Fassaden sind durch die Fensteröffnungen bestimmt, die Gestalt untersteht den Ordnungsprinzipien dieser Architektur: den Horizontalen des Blockbaus, den Vertikalen der Fensteröffnungen. Das Dekor wirkt oft üppig – es hilft aber mit, die grauen Wintertage zu überstehen.

Tomsk ist ein Beispiel für kollektives Gestalten und in Gemeinschaft entstandene Werke. Jedes einzelne Haus hat darin seine eigene Aussage, die bis in die heutige Zeit verstanden wird: Es ist der spontane Ausdruck für die Suche nach dem Glück.

Werner Blaser widmet sich unablässig der weltweiten Suche nach den Zusammenhängen zwischen Material und Struktur. Er läßt uns hier von neuem Zeuge dieses Wirkens werden.

Introduction

Architecture is life, and as such it is intimately related to people. Great cultures therefore have a determining influence on building and create an architecture of their own. A major role is played not only by the will to produce style and form, but also by a knowledge of materials, technical expertise, familiarity with building regulations, manual skills and a sense of responsibility. Architecture has always had a cultural significance as a specific expression of the political, economic and intellectual character of whole eras. At the same time it performs an important social function. A mode of construction adapted to the available materials, the prevailing climate and the existing technical knowledge and ability makes a substantial contribution to the development of a region. Architecture thus becomes a mirror of history.

As a result of the collapse of the communist system, the Siberian town of Tomsk, which for decades was closed to foreign visitors, has come nearer to us in the architectural sense as well as in other respects. Tomsk is unique in itself: It is a town whose whole character was determined by the architecture of wood, much of whose original substance is still preserved. Only with the present cultural opening of the East has this unique ensemble of wood-built architecture, now more than a century old, been made accessible to us again to demonstrate the close interrelation between material, construction and form.

The main purpose of this book is to promote committed interest in the timber architecture of Tomsk and to reveal the secrets and details of its hitherto unknown buildings. Their high aesthetic standard and the creativity of their architecture, in combination with outstanding craftsmanship, can serve as a model to us for the buildings we erect today. Precisely for this reason, major efforts must be undertaken without delay to preserve this architectural ensemble from decay.

In Siberia the art of building in wood experienced a dynamic development, and from the 16th century onwards evolved its own, regional characteristics. The foundations of the timber architecture of this region were its vast forests and extreme climatic conditions. In centuries of practical experience, particularly in the 18th and 19th centuries, local carpenters developed a building tradition which had not only a technical but also a truly artistic character. The results are unique architectural testimonies in which ornamentation is integrated into the overall composition of the building. It is to its filigree ornamentation that this architecture, whose character is determined by its material, owes its uniqueness.

Wood-built houses in Tomsk – yesterday and today

Tomsk was founded in 1604 when Russian soldiers built a fort from logs on a hill overlooking the Tomsk river. A hundred years later, when the fortifications were no longer needed, a wooden church was built on the same site. In 1782 Tomsk, which had been a place of exile since the 17th century, became the district capital of Western Siberia. As a result of its good communications by land and water, the town grew into an important centre of commerce. A census in 1804 showed Tomsk to have 6776 inhabitants and 1508 buildings of which only three were of stone and the remainder of wood. Unfortunately, as a result of disastrous fires no buildings from that period have survived.

The log buildings of that time were plain and undecorated. The town was constructed on a grid pattern with single-storey houses. Around 1830, an urban planner from St. Petersburg developed a fan-shaped layout for the streets. During that period, buildings were constructed with a more urban character which nonetheless bore the mark of Russian traditions. These houses with three to five windows were built so that their narrow side faced onto the street while the side at right angles to it, with the entrance, faced onto the yard. Because of the danger of fire with houses of wood, a spacing of 25 metres between buildings was stipulated. Towards the end of the 19th century, as a result of the growing prosperity of the town and particularly of its merchants, wooden ornamentation made its appearance. Windows, pilasters and cornices were decorated so as to stand out in contrast from the log structure.

In 1896 Tomsk was connected to a branch line of the Trans-Siberian Railway and a railway office building was erected there. Whereas the early inhabitants of the town had been mainly farmers who lived modestly and almost on the verge of poverty, shortly before the turn of the century the foundation of the first university in Siberia brought an influx of academics, artists and architects. This gave a major stimulus to the local timber architecture with its unique style of decoration.

Many of the architectural works of art that were created at that time are still in existence today; they bear the mark of the "Art Nouveau" style which appeared on the scene at the beginning of the 20th century. An important figure during this period was the painter and architect V. Ortseshko. He was responsible for designing many of the wooden buildings that are now under preservation orders. At that time in Tomsk it was possible to serve a two-year course of training at a vocational school. This course, with around a hundred students, covered all the constructional and decorative elements of house building and wood architecture. Most of the wooden houses in Tomsk that are still inhabited date from this period.

In the second half of our century, with the progressive industrialisation of western Siberia, the traditional mode of building in wood was abandoned. Due to the rapid growth of the population in Tomsk – today a city of half a million people – the mainly two-storeyed wooden houses often had to make way for bigger apartment blocks. The mineral-rich region around Tomsk has now developed into an important industrial, administrative and cultural centre. However, as a result of the difficulties of reconstructing the Russian economy it is again suffering from a shortage of food and everyday necessities.

Seen against this background, the wood-built houses of Tomsk impressively illustrate the level of accomplishment achieved by Russian carpenters and are an enduring sign of a creativity that is only gradually beginning to develop again in the political and economic life of the country. The buildings documented by the Tomsk authority for the protection of monuments – roughly 1000 in number – are unique in Western culture. In them we can find a building culture, lost to our part of the world, that is rooted in a close-knit social structure. At the same time they illustrate, in a new dimension, the fusion between structure and style. Precisely for this reason, to view these wooden buildings and to appreciate this unique architecture can for us be like a promise.

Tomsk can thus be regarded as a fabulous treasure trove that represents a turning point in simple peasant architecture: The arrangement and profiling of window units in the facade of traditional log buildings. Masterfully decorated windows are placed like jewels in front of the log facade, and form a rectangular frame for pictures poetic in their charm. Then, as the finishing touch, comes the cornice. Each of the three chapters of this book is devoted to one of these elements in the facade: the log structure, the cladding, the cornice.

Introduction

Tomsk: une architecture bois inconnue

L'architecture est vie; elle est ainsi étroitement associée aux hommes. Les grandes cultures impriment donc leur marque jusque dans la construction, en produisant leur propre architecture. Certes, une volonté formelle et le choix d'un style s'y expriment, mais l'intelligence des matériaux, le savoir-faire technique, la connaissance des règlements de construction, l'habileté artisanale et le sentiment d'être responsable y jouent aussi un rôle primordial. Expression spécifique de la situation politique, économique et intellectuelle d'une époque, l'architecture a toujours une dimension culturelle. En même temps, elle remplit une fonction sociale importante. Un mode de construire adapté aux matériaux disponibles, aux conditions climatiques et au savoirfaire existant est un facteur essentiel de développement pour une région. L'architecture devient alors le miroir de l'histoire.

Le système socialiste ayant disparu, se sont ouvertes devant nous les portes d'une ville sibérienne interdite pendant des dizaines d'années, et donc de son architecture: Tomsk et ses maisons en bois. Tomsk est un cas tout à fait unique en son genre: l'architecture bois y est présente dans toute la ville, et l'on y retrouve aujourd'hui encore de nombreux témoignages d'un art de bâtir vieux de plus d'un siècle. Il aura fallu attendre l'ouverture à l'Est pour que cette production architecturale exceptionnelle se présente à nous dans les rapports profonds qu'entretiennent entre eux le matériau, la structure et la forme.

Puisse ce livre éveiller les sensibilités et encourager les engagements en faveur de l'architecture bois de Tomsk. Il montre les secrets et les détails de constructions ignorées jusqu'à ce jour, alors que leur beauté remarquable et leur architecture si créative, associées à une extrême habileté artisanale, pourraient inspirer notre architecture d'aujourd'hui. Mais des mesures rapides et importantes sont nécessaires pour sauver de la ruine qui le menace cet ensemble sibérien véritablement unique.

En Sibérie, l'architecture bois a manifesté une grande vitalité dès le XVIe siècle, se développant avec ses propres particularités d'une région à une autre. Elle y a été encouragée par la présence de forêts immenses et par des conditions climatiques extrêmes. Héritiers d'une pratique séculaire, les charpentiers des XVIIIe et XIXe siècles surtout ont alors développé non seulement leur technique de construction, mais encore une véritable tradition architecturale. C'est ainsi que sont nés des témoignages architecturaux uniques, intégrant à la perfection l'ornement dans le bâti, avec la singularité de leurs décors en filigrane.

Maisons en bois de Tomsk – hier et aujourd'hui

Tomsk a été fondée en 1604 sur une colline, au bord de la rivière Tom: des soldats russes bâtirent là une place forte en rondins. Cent ans plus tard, la fortification n'étant plus utilisée, on édifia à la place une église en bois. En 1782, Tomsk, devenue aussi lieu d'exil depuis le XVIIe siècle, est un chef-lieu d'arrondissement de la Sibérie occidentale. Jouissant de bonnes communications par mer et par terre, elle devient un important centre de commerce. En 1804, un recensement de la population y dénombre 6776 habitants et 1508 bâtiments, dont trois seulement sont en pierre et tous les autres en bois. Malheureusement, l'incendie y a fait des ravages et aucun ouvrage ne nous est resté de cette époque.

Les constructions d'alors, en rondins et en madriers, étaient sobres, sans ornements. La ville suivait un plan rectiligne, les maisons n'avaient qu'un étage. En 1830, un architecte venu de Saint-Pétersbourg dessine des artères en éventail. Des constructions d'allure plus citadine apparaissent alors, au style cependant marqué par la tradition russe. Comportant trois à cinq fenêtres, ces maisons présentent sur la rue leur côté étroit, tandis que leur entrée et leur longue façade sont tournées côté cour. Compte tenu d'un risque d'incendie accru avec des constructions en bois, celles-ci doivent être espacées d'au moins 25 mètres. C'est vers la fin du XIXe siècle, la prospérité grandissant, essentiellement parmi les commerçants, que les premiers ornements en bois apparaissent sur les maisons. Fenêtres, pilastres et corniches se font décorations, contrastant vivement avec le fond de bois massif.

En 1896, une ligne secondaire du chemin de fer sibérien arrive jusqu'à Tomsk. L'administration ferroviaire s'y construit un bâtiment. Avec la fondation de la première université de Sibérie, au début du siècle, les scientifiques, les artistes et les architectes affluent vers la ville. Cette nouvelle population, mêlée à celle constituée en majorité de paysans vivant modestement, sinon pauvrement, amène un essor important de l'architecture locale en bois, avec les décors qui lui sont propres.

De grands ouvrages sont alors créés à Tomsk, dont un certain nombre ont été conservés jusqu'à ce jour; ils sont marqués par le style Art Nouveau né au début du XXe siècle. A cette époque, V. Orzheshko, peintre et architecte, dessine bon nombre des maisons qui sont aujourd'hui placées sous la sauvegarde de la Conservation des monuments. Une école dispense une formation de deux ans en architecture bois, incluant tous les éléments d'une construction et de sa décoration. Elle compte une centaine d'élèves. C'est de cette période que datent la plupart des maisons en bois qui sont encore habitées actuellement.

Dès la deuxième moitié de notre siècle, la construction en bois traditionnelle disparaît peu à peu dans le courant d'industrialisation qui déferle sur la Sibérie occidentale. Tomsk connaît un rapide développement démographique – la ville compte aujourd'hui un demi-million d'habitants – et les maisons en bois, le plus souvent à deux étages, ont souvent dû céder la place à des ensembles d'habitation plus vastes. Autour de la ville, le sol est riche en ressources et la région est devenue un important centre industriel, administratif et culturel. Aujourd'hui cependant, vu les difficultés de la reconstruction économique, il y a pénurie de vivres et de produits de base.

Sur la toile de fond que tissent les problèmes économiques, les maisons en bois de Tomsk sont d'autant plus impressionnantes par l'art consommé de l'artisan charpentier qu'elles révèlent et par le signe visible et permanent qu'elles constituent d'une créativité qui recommence seulement à profiter peu à peu à la vie politique et économique du pays. Les bâtiments recensés par la Conservation des monuments de Tomsk – un millier – sont uniques dans la culture occidentale. En eux, nous renouons avec un fond architectural qui, chez nous, a disparu; il trouve ses racines dans un tissu social dense et représente à nos yeux une dimension nouvelle de la croissance osmotique entre structure et forme. La découverte et l'observation de cette architecture bois si particulière nous sont comme une promesse.

De Tomsk on retiendra une fabuleuse découverte ainsi qu'une trouvaille qui représente un tournant dans la simple architecture paysanne: l'arrangement et la mise en relief d'ensembles de fenêtres sur fond de façade en bois massif, éléments précieux appliqués sur une surface en rondins ou en madriers, formant une figure géométrique charmante et poétique. Et pour parfaire le tout, la couronne en bois. Cette composition de façade dicte les trois parties de ce livre: la construction en rondins ou en madriers, le revêtement, la couronne.

Unbekannte sibirische Holzbaukunst

Architektur ist Leben und mit den Menschen verbunden. Große Kulturen prägen deshalb auch das Bauen und bringen so eine eigene Architektur hervor. Nicht allein der Form- und Stilwille, sondern auch Materialkenntnisse, technisches Wissen, Kenntnisse der Bauvorschriften, handwerkliche Fähigkeiten und Verantwortungsgefühl spielen hier eine wesentliche Rolle. Als spezifischer Ausdruck der politischen, wirtschaftlichen und geistigen Situation ganzer Epochen hat Architektur immer eine kulturelle Bedeutung. Sie erfüllt aber gleichzeitig auch eine wichtige soziale Funktion. Eine Bauweise, die den verfügbaren Materialien, dem herrschenden Klima und dem technischen Wissen und Können angepaßt ist, trägt wesentlich zur Entwicklung einer Region bei. Architektur wird so zum Spiegel der Geschichte.

Der Zusammenbruch des real existierenden Sozialismus hat uns die sibirische Stadt Tomsk, welche über Jahrzehnte eine geschlossene Stadt war, auch in architektonischer Hinsicht wieder näher gebracht. Tomsk stellt eine Besonderheit eigener Art dar: Die Holzbaukunst hat hier eine ganze Stadt geprägt, und vieles von der alten Bausubstanz ist bis heute erhalten geblieben. Erst mit der heutigen kulturellen Öffnung des Ostens wurden die Kulissen dieser über ein Jahrhundert alten Holzbaukunst wieder zugänglich, und so vermag uns dieses einmalige Ensemble die tiefen Zusammenhänge zwischen Material, Konstruktion und Form vor Augen zu führen.

Das Hauptanliegen dieses Buches ist es, für die Holzarchitektur von Tomsk die Aufgeschlossenheit engagierter Interessenten zu fördern und die Geheimnisse und Details der bisher unbekannten Bauten darzustellen. Ihre bewundernswerte Schönheit und baukünstlerische Kreativität, gepaart mit großem handwerklichen Geschick, können uns Vorbild sein auch für unser heutiges Bauen. Gerade deshalb sind große und schnelle Anstrengungen vonnöten, um dieses architektonische Ensemble in Sibirien vor dem drohenden Verfall zu retten.

In Sibirien entfaltete die Holzbaukunst eine große Vitalität und entwickelte sich dort seit dem 16. Jahrhundert mit ihren eigenen, regionalen Besonderheiten. Mächtige Waldbestände und extreme Klimabedingungen waren die Grundlagen dieser spezifischen Holzarchitektur. Aus jahrhundertealter Praxis entwickelten die Zimmerleute, hauptsächlich im 18. und 19. Jahrhundert, nicht nur eine bautechnische, sondern eine eigentlich baukünstlerische Tradition. So entstanden einzigartige architektonische Zeugnisse, bei denen das Zierwerk in der Gesamtkomposition der Baumasse integriert wurde. Das Besondere an dieser materialgeprägten Architektur sind ihre filigranen Dekors.

Holzhäuser in Tomsk – gestern und heute

Auf einem über dem Fluß Tomsk gelegenen Hügel wurde Tomsk 1604 gegründet: russische Soldaten bauten damals eine Festung aus Rundhölzern. Hundert Jahre später, als die Befestigungsanlage nicht mehr benötigt wurde, errichtete man an der gleichen Stelle eine Holzkirche. Im Jahre 1782 wurde Tomsk, das seit dem 17. Jahrhundert auch ein Verbannungsort war, westsibirische Kreishauptstadt. Durch die guten Verkehrsverbindungen auf dem Land- und auch auf dem Wasserweg wuchs die Stadt zu einem bedeutenden Handelszentrum heran. Bei einer Volkszählung im Jahre 1804 wurden in Tomsk 6'776 Einwohner und 1'508 Gebäude gezählt, davon nur drei aus Stein, alle übrigen aus Holz. Leider sind aus dieser Zeit aufgrund von Feuersbrünsten keine Bauwerke mehr erhalten geblieben.

Die Blockbauten waren damals schlicht und ohne Dekoration. Der Stadtplan war auf eine rechtwinklige Straßenführung mit einstöckigen Häusern ausgerichtet. Um 1830 entwickelte dann ein Stadtplaner aus St. Petersburg ein fächerförmiges System für die Straßen. In dieser Zeit entstanden Bauten in einem mehr städtischen, aber doch durch russische Traditionen geprägten Stil. Diese Häuser mit drei bis fünf Fenstern waren mit ihrer Schmalseite gegen die Straße ausgerichtet, die Quer- und Eingangsseite öffnete sich gegen den Hof. Wegen erhöhter Brandgefahr bei Holzhäusern wurde der Gebäudeabstand auf 25 Meter festgelegt. Gegen Ende des 19. Jahrhunderts hielt, begründet durch den ansteigenden Wohlstand vor allem der Kaufleute, der dekorative Holzschmuck beim Hausbau Einzug. Fenster, Lisenen und Dachgesims wurden verziert und derart kontrastreich vom Holzblock abgehoben.

1896 wurde Tomsk an eine Nebenlinie der sibirischen Eisenbahn angeschlossen, ein Eisenbahn-Bürogebäude wurde errichtet. Während in Tomsk zunächst mehrheitlich Bauern bescheiden und fast ärmlich ihr Leben führten, kamen kurz vor der Jahrhundertwende im Zuge der ersten Universitätsgründung Sibiriens Wissenschaftler, Künstler und Architekten in die Stadt. Dadurch erhielt auch die örtliche Holzarchitektur mit ihrem spezifischen Dekor einen bedeutenden Aufschwung.

Viele dieser damals entstandenen großartigen architektonischen Kunstwerke sind uns bis heute erhalten geblieben; sie sind vom anfangs des 20. Jahrhunderts aufgekommenen «Art-Nouveau»-Stil geprägt. Ein bedeutender Mann aus dieser Epoche war der Maler und Architekt V. Orzheshko. Aus seiner Hand stammt eine Vielzahl von Entwürfen der heute denkmalgeschützten Holzhäuser. Damals gab es in Tomsk auch die Möglichkeit, eine zweijährige Ausbildung an einer Fachschule zu absolvieren. Es wurde ein Lehrprogramm mit allen konstruktiven und dekorativen Elementen des Hausbaus und der Holzbaukunst angeboten; man zählte einhundert Schüler. Auf diese Zeit gehen die meisten der heute noch bewohnten Holzhäuser in Tomsk zurück.

In der zweiten Hälfte unseres Jahrhunderts wurde im Zuge der Industrialisierung von Westsibirien die traditionelle Holzbauweise nicht mehr angewendet. Die schnelle Bevölkerungsentwicklung in Tomsk – heute leben in dieser Großstadt eine halbe Million Einwohner – hatte außerdem zur Folge, daß die mehrheitlich zweigeschossigen Holzhäuser oft größeren Wohnblocks weichen mußten. Inzwischen hat sich die an Bodenschätzen reiche Region um Tomsk zu einem bedeutenden Industrie-, Verwaltungs- und Kulturzentrum entwickelt. Doch aufgrund der Schwierigkeiten des wirtschaftlichen Wiederaufbaus fehlt es auch jetzt wieder an Lebensmitteln und einfachen Produkten.

Vor diesem Hintergrund sind die Holzhäuser in Tomsk ein beeindruckendes Beispiel vollendeter russischer Zimmermannskunst und damit das sichtbare und bleibende Zeichen einer Kreativität, die sich in der Politik und der Wirtschaft des Landes erst wieder allmählich zu entfalten vermag: Die von der Denkmalpflege in Tomsk dokumentierten Bauten – etwa 1000 an der Zahl – sind in der abendländischen Kultur einzigartig. In ihnen finden wir eine bei uns verloren gegangene Baukultur, welche in einem enggewobenen sozialen Gefüge wurzelt, und gleichzeitig eine neue Dimension des Zusammenwachsens von Struktur und Gestalt. Gerade deshalb kann das Betrachten und das Erkennen dieser besonderen Holzbaukunst für uns wie ein Versprechen sein.

Es ist also von Tomsk als einem fabelhaften Fund zu berichten, von einer Trouvaille, die eine Wende im einfachen bäuerlichen Bauen darstellt: Das Arrangieren und Profilieren von Fenstereinheiten in der Fassadengestalt der traditionellen Blockbauweise. Wie ein Juwel sind gekonnt dekorierte Fenster vor die Holzblockfassade gestellt und bilden ein lieblich und poetisch Rahmenviereck von Bildern. Dazu kommt als Abschluß der Dachkranz. Dieser Fassadengliederung entsprechen die drei Kapitel des Buches: der Blockbau, die Verschalung, der Kranz.

Tomsk, one of the oldest towns in
Siberia, is located roughly 200 km
to the north of Novosibirsk.
Originally a stronghold, Tomsk
developed into a town of rich
merchants. Today it is a major
centre of industry, culture,
education and commerce. The
illustration shows the town as it
was in the 17th century.

Tomsk, l'une des plus anciennes
villes de Sibérie, se trouve à
quelque 200 km au nord de
Novossibirsk. Construite sur les
lieux d'une ancienne fortification,
elle a été une cité de riches
commerçants. Aujourd'hui, Tomsk
est un grand centre industriel,
culturel et économique. Ici, la ville
telle qu'elle était au XVIIᵉ siècle.

Tomsk, eine der ältesten Städte
Sibiriens, liegt etwa 200 km
nördlich von Novosibirsk. Aus einer
Befestigungsanlage entstand eine
Stadt reicher Kaufleute. Heute ist
Tomsk ein großes Industrie-,
Kultur-, Bildungs- und
Wirtschaftszentrum. Die Abbildung
zeigt die Stadt im 17. Jahrhundert.

Model of a district of Tomsk which
is to be transformed into a
"museum". According to the plans
of the "Spezproiektrestavratsia"
Institute in Tomsk, people are to
live here as at the end of the
19th century, businesses are to be
activated and the whole district is to
be restored to its original
appearance.

Maquette d'un quartier de Tomsk,
destiné à être transformé en
«musée»: un projet de restauration
de l'Institut Spezprojektrestawrazia
à Tomsk prévoit en effet de faire ici
vivre et travailler les gens, comme
à la fin du XIXe siècle.

Modell von einem Stadtbezirk in
Tomsk, der in ein «Museum»
verwandelt werden soll:
Nach den Plänen des Instituts
«Spezprojektrestawrazia» in Tomsk
sollen hier – wie am Ende des
19. Jahrhunderts – Menschen
wohnen, Geschäfte aktiviert und
alles in seiner ursprünglichen
Gestalt restauriert werden.

The log structure – the basis

Wood as a building material

The area around the town of Tomsk, a region with a long tradition of using wood, is richly timbered. The trees occurring there include the silver and downy birch, the Scots pine, Arolla pine, Siberian spruce and Siberian larch. It is above all the endless coniferous forests of the Siberian plain that provide the raw material for the fascinating two-storeyed buildings in the vernacular round log form of construction. The construction material was provided primarily by larch and spruce trunks in the form of logs, squared beams and planks. The beams for the log walls were hewn and sawn from tall, straight-trunked trees. This type of log construction is to be seen mainly in eastern and northern regions, but also in the Alps at the timber line. The required building material is obtained from the long, straight trunks of coniferous trees from the forests that grow there. The harsh climate is particularly suited to log construction. The trees were felled in the autumn when they were no longer in sap. The barked logs were able to dry out during the winter, and the spring was a good time to build.

These log structures had been widespread in Norway, Sweden and also in Russia since the time of the Vikings, from c. 800 to 1000 AD. At the beginning of the Middle Ages, in the 13th and 14th centuries, the construction of log dwelling houses played an important role in Siberia. The Russian culture of the time, including church art, was primarily of Byzantine origin. There was also a tradition of building in wood in Byzantine Constantinople; the villas on the Bosporus were built mainly from this noble material. In Siberia, log construction was used even for church and chapel architecture.

Log construction is a simple and rapid way of building: The walls are formed of the trunks of coniferous trees, laid horizontally upon each other after appropriate preparation in their cross-section and length. The ends of these trunks are recessed so as to interlock at right angles as the walls are built up. In contrast to the mainly single-storeyed buildings of Scandinavia, most of the log-built houses in Tomsk in Siberia were of two or more storeys.

The log system of construction

The log buildings of Tomsk can be divided into two broad categories: pure log buildings and clad log buildings. These types differ little in their basic construction. The system of building solid walls from tree trunks placed horizontally upon each other in the form of round logs, squared beams or halved logs exhibits a wide variety of coggings in the corner joints with protruding beam ends. However, the master carpenters of Tomsk were also adept at making corner joints without protruding ends by techniques such as dovetailing and halving.

The timber houses of Tomsk thus reflect a deep-rooted tradition of log construction. But it is only through their further development that these houses acquired a special character: Ornamented windows and decorative elements made from wood are applied to the facades. The wooden ornaments are cut out of simple boards. The houses are also crowned with an impressive cornice. It is this artistic decoration which accounts for the uniqueness of Tomsk and its wood architecture, and which still today evokes a feeling of respect and admiration in the Western visitor.

Roughly a thousand of these picturesque houses which were formerly inhabited by merchants, mainly fur dealers, are still in existence. Today they serve principally as dwellings for working class people. Ornamented with all kinds of votive gifts, these houses with their fragile decor on wooden boards are a testimony to the art of conjuring up beauty out of nothing. The ornamental window is pleasing to the eye and evokes an aesthetic mood of its own. One is fascinated by the delicate wooden shapes on the frieze with its organic lines, pastel tones and shadow effect. Here architecture and the dwelling environment are the expression of a feeling for life long perished in our own regions but still present here in the visual experience of these decorative details.

L'élémentaire – la construction en rondins ou en madriers

Le bois comme matériau de construction

Autour de Tomsk, la contrée est riche en forêts et le paysage est traditionnellement marqué par le bois. Le bouleau, le pin sylvestre et l'arole y côtoient l'épicéa et le mélèze sibériens. Ce sont les forêts de résineux s'étendant à l'infini dans la plaine sibérienne qui fournissent principalement la matière première des constructions traditionnelles à deux étages, en rondins, en madriers ou en planches pris dans des grumes de mélèze et d'épicéa. Les arbres hauts de tronc, poussés droit, étaient taillés à la hache et sciés pour les poutres destinées aux parois. Cette technique de construction en rondins ou en madriers se rencontre principalement dans les régions orientales et septentrionales, mais aussi dans les Alpes, à la limite supérieure des forêts. Mais la saine construction en rondins ou en madriers était aussi adaptée à la rudesse du climat. On abattait les arbres en automne, alors que le bois n'était plus en sève. Les grumes écorcées pouvaient sécher pendant l'hiver. Le printemps était la saison favorable pour construire les maisons.

Les constructions en rondins et en madriers se répandent en Norvège, en Suède et en Russie depuis l'époque des Vikings, c'est-à-dire entre 800 et 1000 après Jésus-Christ. Au début du Moyen Age – XIIIe et XIVe siècle –, les habitations en rondins et en madriers jouent un rôle important en Sibérie. La culture russe d'alors, même l'ecclésiastique, est d'origine essentiellement byzantine. Dans la Constantinople byzantine aussi, la construction en bois est de tradition ancienne, et c'est dans ce noble matériau que sont construites la plupart des villas situées sur les rives du Bosphore. En Sibérie, même les églises et les chapelles sont construites en rondins et en madriers.

La technique est simple et rapide: des grumes de résineux, superposées à l'horizontale et mises à dimension en section et en longueur, forment les parois de la maison. Les extrémités des grumes sont entaillées et emboîtées les unes dans les autres au fur et à mesure que montent les parois assemblées à angle droit. A Tomsk, c'est ainsi qu'on a construit des maisons comportant le plus souvent deux étages, voire davantage; en Scandinavie, en revanche, ce type de construction est en général plus «plat».

Rondins ou madriers, un système de construction

Les constructions typiques de Tomsk se divisent en deux catégories: celles qui sont seulement en rondins ou en madriers, et celles qui comportent un revêtement. Structuralement, il n'y a guère de différence. A l'intérieur du système qui consiste à superposer des grumes – bois ronds ou demi-ronds ou bois équarris –, on trouve en revanche toute une palette d'assemblages à paume, avec têtes de poutres saillantes, ou à enfourchement et à mi-bois, sans poutres saillantes; les uns et les autres étaient parfaitement maîtrisés par les charpentiers indigènes.

Les maisons en bois de Tomsk que nous connaissons aujourd'hui se réfèrent par conséquent à la tradition profondément enracinée de la maison en rondins et en madriers. Elles ne présentent un caractère véritablement spécifique qu'à partir du moment où leurs façades s'ornent de fenêtres en applique ou d'éléments décoratifs en bois, découpés à la scie dans de simples planches. Lorsque s'y ajoute la remarquable couronne de toiture, l'ornementation est complète et l'architecture bois de Tomsk prend ce caractère unique et particulier qui suscite toujours, chez le visiteur occidental, le respect et l'admiration.

Des habitations pittoresques dans lesquelles vivaient jadis des commerçants – négociants en fourrures surtout –, il en reste aujourd'hui près d'un millier, dans lesquelles habitent des ouvriers. Avec leurs motifs votifs de toutes sortes, elles témoignent du don artistique capable de créer la beauté d'un coup de baguette magique, grâce à un fragile décor en planches de bois. Plaisir des yeux, la fenêtre en applique apporte une dimension esthétique. Avec leurs lignes organiques, leurs tons pastel et leurs effets d'ombre et de lumière, les ornementations de la couronne de toiture exercent une véritable fascination. Architecture et forme d'habitat sont ici l'expression d'une façon de vivre, depuis longtemps disparue chez nous, mais ici encore présente, dans le vécu visuel de ces détails d'ornement.

Der Holzblockbau – das Elementare

Baumaterial Holz

Reich an Wald ist die Gegend rund um die Stadt Tomsk, eine von alter Holztradition geprägte Landschaft. Dort kommen als Baumarten die Weiß- und Moorbirke, die Waldkiefer und die Arve sowie die sibirische Fichte und die sibirische Lärche vor. Vor allem die endlosen Nadelwälder der sibirischen Ebene liefern den Rohstoff für die faszinierenden zweistöckigen Rundholzbauten in volkstümlicher Blockhaustechnik. Als Bauholz fanden insbesondere die Stämme von Lärchen und Fichten Verwendung, und zwar als Rundholz, als Vierkantbalken und als Bretter. Aus hochstämmigen geraden Bäumen wurden die Blockwandbalken gehauen und gesägt. Diese Blockbautechnik ist hauptsächlich in östlichen und nördlichen Gebieten zu finden, aber auch in den Alpen an der oberen Waldgrenze. Aus den gerade wachsenden, langen Nadelholzstämmen der dortigen Wälder wird das dafür notwendige Baumaterial gewonnen. Aber auch dem rauhen Klima kommt der gesunde Holzblockbau entgegen. Die Bäume wurden im Herbst gefällt, wenn das Holz nicht mehr im Saft stand. Im Winter konnten die entrindeten Stämme austrocknen, und das Frühjahr war eine gute Zeit für den Hausbau.

Seit der Wikingerzeit, etwa von 800–1000 n. Chr., fand in Norwegen, Schweden und auch in Rußland die Verbreitung dieser Blockbauten statt. Zu Beginn des Mittelalters, im 13./14. Jahrhundert, spielte der Blockwohnbau in Sibirien eine wichtige Rolle. Die damalige russische Kultur, einschließlich der Kirchenkunst, war in erster Linie byzantinischen Ursprungs. Auch im byzantinischen Konstantinopel hatte die Holzbauweise Tradition; dort wurden die Villen am Bosporus größtenteils aus diesem edlen Material gebaut. In Sibirien wurde der Blockbau sogar für die Kirchen- und Kapellenarchitektur genutzt.

Der Blockbau mit Holz ist eine einfache und schnelle Bauweise: Waagrecht übereinandergelegte, in Querschnitt und Länge entsprechend vorbereitete Nadelholzstämme bilden die Wände. Die Enden dieser Stämme werden gekerbt und beim Aufbau der rechtwinklig aufeinanderstossenden Wände ineinander verkeilt. Mit dieser Blockbautechnik wurden – im Gegensatz zu den überwiegenden Flachbauten Skandinaviens – im sibirischen Tomsk meist Häuser mit zwei oder mehreren Stockwerken gebaut.

Der Blockbau als Konstruktionssystem

In Tomsk sind grundsätzlich zwei Typen von Blockbauten zu finden: reine Blockbauten und verschalte Blockbauten. Konstruktiv unterscheiden sich diese Bautypen kaum. Das Bausystem, das aus einheitlichen Blockwänden waagrecht aufeinander gelegter Baumstämme in Form von Rundhölzern, Vierkantbalken oder Halbhölzern besteht, zeigt eine Vielfalt von Verkämmungen der Eckverbände mit überstehenden Balkenköpfen. Aber auch die nicht überstehenden Eckverbände wie Verzinkung und Verblattung wurden von den Tomsker Zimmermeistern beherrscht.

So verweisen die Holzhäuser in Tomsk auf eine tief verwurzelte Bautradition des Blockhausbaus. Doch erst deren Weiterentwicklung ist das Besondere dieser Bauten: Auf die Fassaden sind vorgesetzte Fenster sowie dekorative Elemente aus Holz appliziert. Es handelt sich um dekorativ wirkende Holzelemente, welche aus einfachen Brettern ausgesägt wurden. Zudem sind die Häuser jeweils mit einem sehenswerten Dachkranz gekrönt. Erst diese kunstvollen Dekorationen machen aus Tomsk und seiner Holzbaukunst etwas Besonderes, und sie rufen auch noch heute beim westlichen Besucher ein Gefühl des Respekts und der Bewunderung hervor.

Von den malerischen Wohnhäusern, in denen einst Kaufleute, meist Pelzhändler, lebten, sind immer noch rund tausend übriggeblieben. Sie dienen heute überwiegend Arbeitern als Wohnraum. Mit allerlei Votivgaben verziert, zeugen diese Häuser von der künstlerischen Gabe, durch ein fragiles Dekor auf Holzbrettern das Schöne aus dem Nichts hervorzuzaubern. Das vor die Fassade gesetzte Fenster erfreut das Auge und inszeniert eine ästhetische Stimmung. Faszinierend sind die zierlichen Holzformen am Dachkranz mit ihren organischen Linien, pastellenen Farbtönen und ihrer Schattenwirkung. Architektur und Wohnform sind hier Ausdruck eines Lebensgefühls, das bei uns längst untergegangen ist und das hier – in der visuellen Erlebbarkeit dieser Zierdetails – noch gegenwärtig ist.

The footpath in front of the houses
is screened from the roadway by an
avenue of trees.

Le chemin qui borde les maisons
est protégé de la rue et de sa
circulation par une allée d'arbres.

Der Gehweg vor den Häusern ist
durch eine Baumallee von der
Verkehrsstraße abgeschirmt.

Zones planted with trees between
the log houses.

Bouquets d'arbres entre les
maisons en rondins ou en madriers.

Baumzonen zwischen den
Holzblockbauten.

20

The carved wooden window
surrounds have a slender
appearance that contrasts strongly
with the log facade.

Les encadrements de fenêtre en
bois sculpté, minces et contrastés,
ressortent vivement sur les façades
en rondins ou en madriers.

Die holzgeschnitzten
Fenstereinrahmungen auf der
Blockbaufassade wirken schlank
und kontrastreich.

The narrow side of the houses
generally faces the street, while the
longer side with the house entrance
faces the yard.

Les maisons présentent en général
à la rue leur côté étroit, tandis que
leur longue façade, avec l'entrée de
la maison, donne côté cour.

Die Schmalseite der Häuser liegt
im allgemeinen zur Straße,
während sich die längere Seite mit
dem Hauseingang gegen den Hof
erstreckt.

All outer walls, and also the main internal subdivisions, are in log construction.

Toutes les façades, ainsi que les principales cloisons intérieures, sont construites en rondins ou en madriers.

Sämtliche Fassadenwände und auch die wichtigsten inneren Unterteilungen sind als Blockbau konstruiert.

The division of the window frames,
with their wealth of silhouettes,
resembles a stage backdrop.

Silhouettes en relief et parfum de
coulisses pour les encadrements de
fenêtre.

Kulissenhaft und silhouettenreich
sind die Fenstereinfassungen
gegliedert.

The horizontal alignment of the log structure combines serenity with sternness.

Tout entière à l'horizontale, la structure des façades est aussi paisible que solide.

Die horizontal gerichtete Struktur der Holzfassaden ist so ruhig wie streng.

Order and harmony through slender "ideal" windows of balanced proportions.

Ordre et harmonie grâce à des fenêtres «idéales», élancées et équilibrées.

Ordnung und Harmonie durch schlanke und ausgewogene «ideale» Fenster.

The outer facades set out to give a show of status, whereas the interior appointments of the houses are often very modest.

Les façades extérieures ont été créées pour «se montrer». A l'intérieur des maisons en revanche, l'aménagement est souvent très modeste.

Die Außenfassaden sind auf Repräsentation hin angelegt. Das Innere der Häuser ist dagegen oft sehr bescheiden eingerichtet.

The style of the traditional log building is a reflection of the Siberian forest with its many spruces and larches.

Le style de la construction traditionnelle en rondins ou en madriers est un reflet de la forêt sibérienne, avec ses nombreux épicéas et mélèzes.

Der Baustil des traditionellen Blockbaus spiegelt den sibirischen Wald wider. Dort wachsen Fichten und Lärchen zahlreich.

In years of exposure to the sun, the wood of the log building takes on a dark tone.

Au fil des ans, le soleil donne au bois des rondins et des madriers une coloration plus foncée.

Im Laufe der Jahre färbt die Sonne das Holz des Blockbaus dunkel.

Carving and fretwork in a
decorative window surround.

Décor d'encadrement de fenêtre
sculpté et ciselé à la scie.

Schnitz- und Sägewerk einer
dekorativen Fensterumrahmung.

The surface treatment of the wood
is rich in nuances.

Sur les parties décorées, la surface
du bois a été traitée tout en
nuances.

Im Dekorbereich ist die
Oberflächenbehandlung des Holzes
nuancenreich gestaltet.

32–37
House at Krasnoarmeiskaya 68 in
Tomsk (renovated).

Maison de la Krasnoarmeïskaia 68
à Tomsk (rénovée).

Haus an der Krasnoarmejskaja 68
in Tomsk (renoviert).

The "poetic" forms of this style of
wood construction show influences
from northern Russia.

Les formes «poétiques» de ce style
de construction en bois trahissent
des influences venues du nord de
la Russie.

Die «poetischen» Formen dieses
Holzbaustils zeigen Einflüsse aus
dem Norden Rußlands.

Wall in log construction of round
beams with rhythmically
articulated corner joints.

Paroi en poutres rondes, ponctuée
d'assemblages d'angle bien
rythmés.

Blockbauwand aus Rundbalken mit
rhythmisch gegliederten
Eckverbindungen.

Gable with crested roof ridge.

Pignon à emblème.

Giebel mit kammartigem First.

The white colour of the decorative elements stands out in elegant contrast.

Sur les éléments décoratifs, la couleur blanche crée un contraste précieux.

Kontrastreich und edel wirkt die weiße Farbe der Zierelemente.

План I этажа.

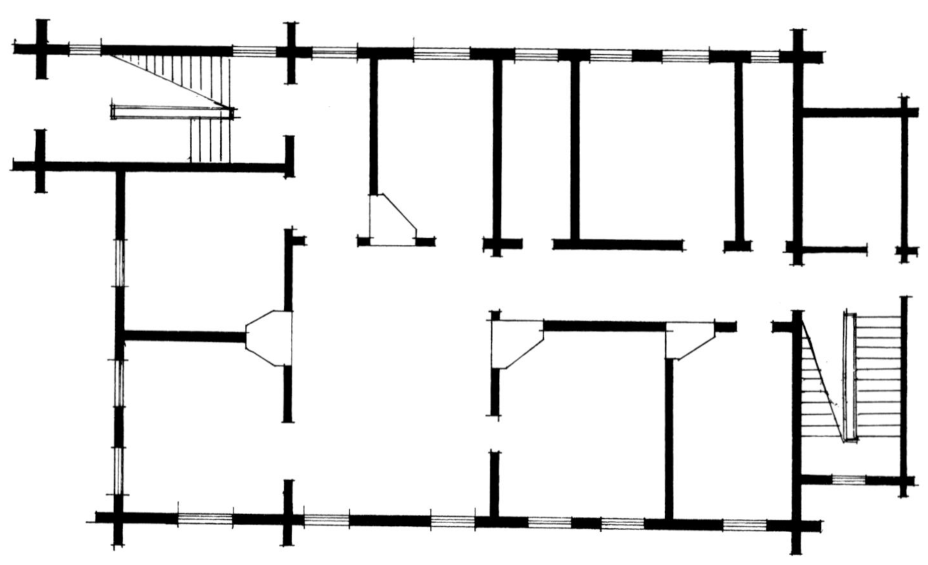

План II этажа.

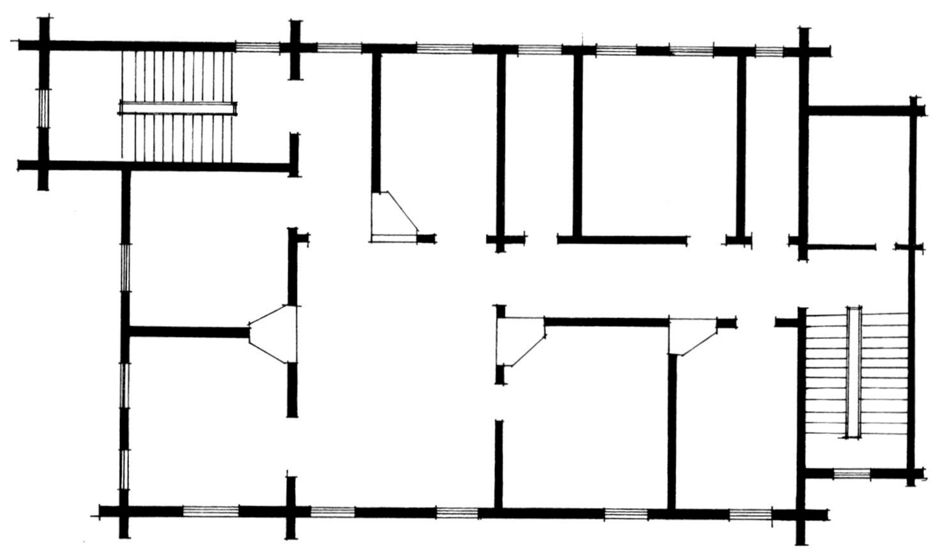

Plans (1:200).

Vue en plan (1:200).

Grundrisse (1:200).

Details of the entrance area.

Details de l'entrée.

 Details der Eingangspartie.

38–43
House on Kirov Prospekt 7 in
Tomsk (renovated).

Maison de la perspective Kirov 7 à
Tomsk (rénovée).

Haus am Kirow Prospekt 7 in
Tomsk (renoviert).

This house was designed by the
Siberian architect Andrei
Dmitrievich Kriatshkov (1880–1950).

Cette maison a été dessinée par
l'architecte sibérien Andreg
Dimitrievitch Kriatchkov
(1880–1950).

Dieses Haus wurde vom
sibirischen Architekten Andreg
Dmitrijewitsch Krjatschkow
(1880–1950) entworfen.

Ornamentation of the timber structure and window details influenced by the "Art Nouveau" style. Balconies were built mainly for such houses.

Les ornementations du bois et les détails de fenêtre portent la marque de l'Art Nouveau. C'est sur ces maisons-là principalement que l'on trouve des balcons.

Vom «Jugendstil» geprägt sind die Verzierungen des Holzblocks und der Fensterdetails. Balkone wurden hauptsächlich bei solchen Häusern gebaut.

Expressively projecting window
elements.

Eléments de fenêtre en
encorbellement.

Ausdrucksvolle auskragende
Fensterelemente.

Oriels were popular "Art Nouveau" motifs.

Les oriels ont été des motifs de prédilection de l'Art Nouveau.

Die Erker waren beliebte Jugendstilmotive.

Elevation (1:100; prior to renovation).

Vue en élévation (1:100; avant rénovation).

Ansicht (1:100; vor der Renovation).

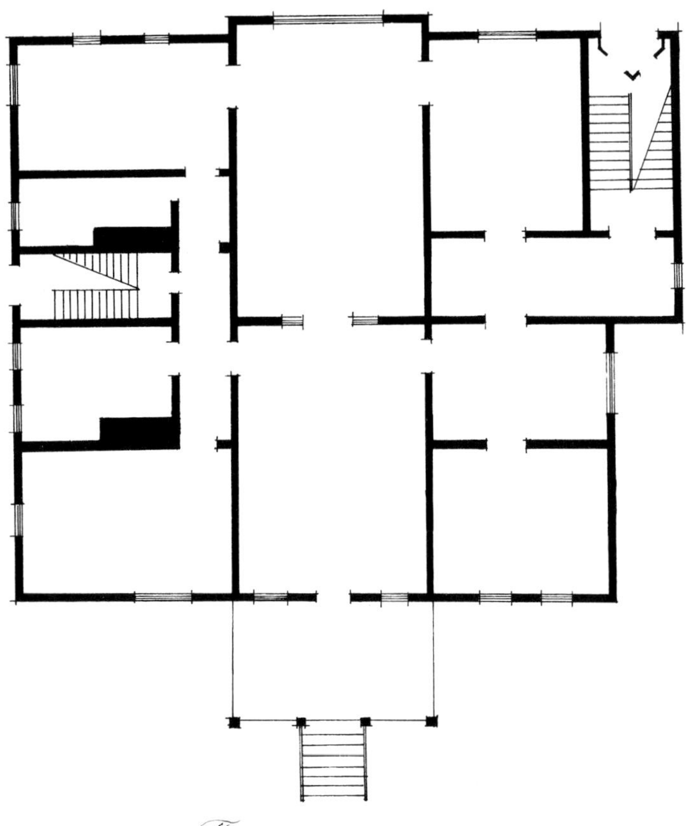

Планъ I этажа.

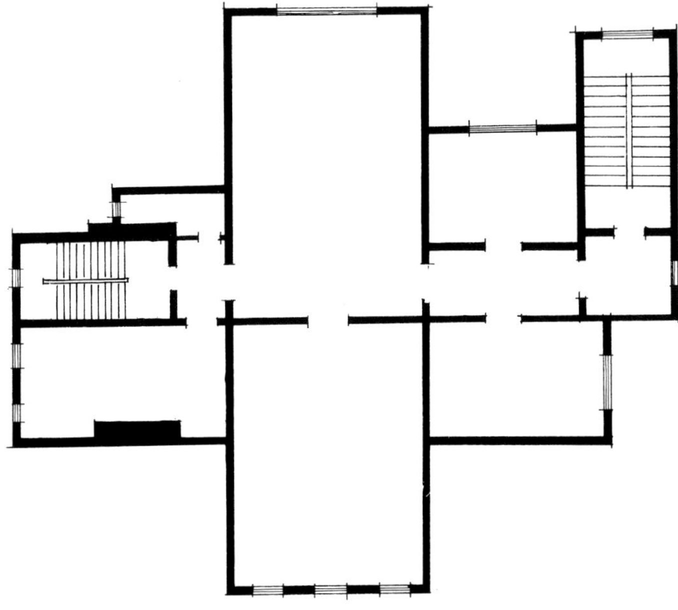

Планъ мансарды.

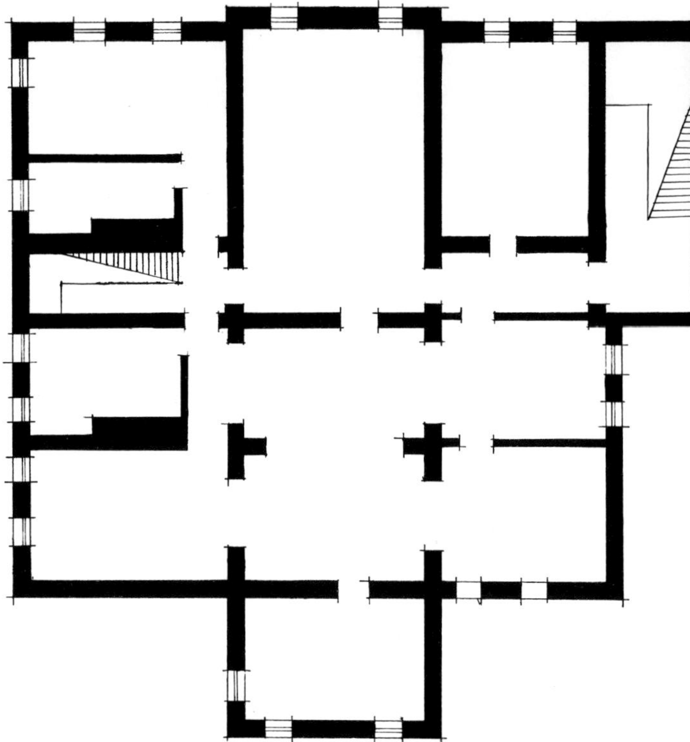

Планъ подвала.

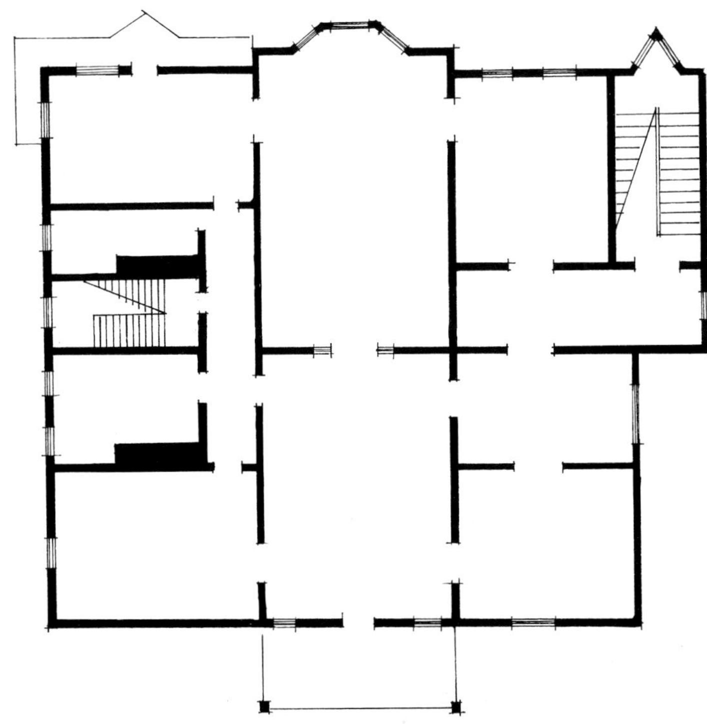

Планъ II этажа.

Plans (1:200).

Vues en plan (1:200).

43 Grundrisse (1:200).

"Baroque" architecture after
Domenico Trezzini (1670–1734) and
Bartolomeo Rastrelli (1700–1771).

Architecture «baroque» selon
Domenico Trezzini (1670–1734) et
Bartolomeo Rastrelli (1700–1771).

«Barock»-Architektur nach
Domenico Trezzini (1670– 1734)
und Bartolomeo Rastrelli
(1700–1771).

The "St. Petersburg" style is also reflected in the window surrounds.

Le «style de Saint-Pétersbourg» se retrouve aussi dans les châssis de fenêtre.

Der «St. Petersburger» Stil spiegelt sich auch in den Fenster-einfassungen wider.

The wood cladding – the fancy dress

The decorated facade

What distinguishes the architecture of Tomsk from customary Russian folk architecture is its fascinating succession of facades. Architecture here is the staging of a window culture: To walk through the streets is like walking through a gallery. Through its combination of inventiveness, the desire for a show of status as well as local style, this "cheerful" architecture evolved a highly effective concept of facade art that contains a multitude of surprises.

The substance of this architectural idea is to be found in the decoration of windows and doors and in the cornice that runs around the roof and the building. At the level of the stone ground floor the facades seem to be built up almost like stage sets, and are thus to be "measured" by the artistry of their openings: The material character and detail of the tall windows, often double and triple windows with large panes, make them into the "crowned opening" which decorates the facade, and consequently into a symbol of all that is festive. The origins of this style of carving are to be found in Byzantium, the Russian Baroque, Classicism and also in Russian folk art. The motifs originate from the world of plants, from ornamental embroidery patterns and also from the theatre. This is truly an architecture that has been taught to dance: The carvings, a favourite element in folk art, adorn the houses in festive garb.

The richly decorated surrounds that typify this window architecture already began to be applied to the log walls before the mid-18th century. The origins of such treasures can be traced to the city of St. Petersburg, the architectural metropolis of the time, where numerous foreign and Russian architects and also thousands of Russian carpenters, joiners and masons were then active. There the Italian architect Bartolomeo Rastrelli (1700–1771) developed magnificent window surrounds as the principal element of his facades. In some respects these facade designs have the character of a mere front, for in most cases the rooms inside the impressive outer facade were quite modest although elegance was lent to them by their generous height.

The building elements of the facades in Tomsk appear to be choreographed; windows placed before the structure shine like gems. In plain wood, or often toned in pastel shades, they are placed in front of the natural-coloured log structure or the toned cladding – always in vertical contrast to the horizontal arrangement of the logs or boards and yet integrated into a complete work of art.

Moving from house to house, through several town quarters, one senses the architecture's link to Tomsk as a locality and as a place of history. Although in need of renovation, these fine town houses, which were originally distributed over the whole town in a chequered pattern, still have a high utility value and still represent a great and unified achievement of urban construction: They embody the unique and artistically outstanding building style of a town as it developed over several centuries.

The ornamented window as a picture frame

The sophisticated arrangement of the window units in the wooden buildings of Tomsk has given rise to a variety of visual effects through the choice of colour and form: Colours and forms are able almost to outwit the eye. At the same time, the wood profiles of the windows are clearly silhouetted against the surface of the facade, and finely outlined motifs with an extreme contrast effect are created. The beauty of this "pearl" of old Siberian wood architecture has an overwhelming ornamental magic. It is an exemplary architecture with a firmly resolute character: The visible structure of these houses, in combination with the will to create a given architectonic form, makes the language of the builder's art readable from the outside.

The embellished windows and doors, and all decorative elements including the ornamental details under the roof, are optimally deployed in the arrangement of the facade. At the same time, the window stands out from the facade as a spatial limitation and thus becomes a symbol of transparency. The uniformly modular character of the whole building results in an unbroken line of harmony. In Tomsk, houses with high and generously proportioned rooms were thus constructed which also fully conform to the needs of the present day.

The view through the tall window is limited by its crossed mullion and transom and its garlands of flowers. If one looks outside from within, or inside from without, one sees a kind of picture. The window forms the frame to this picture. Seen from a greater distance, the window with its ornamental surround also idealises the appearance of the facade – as if it had been embroidered onto its regular surface of solid timber. These openings create a relationship between the inner and the outer world. The window frame thus becomes an element of active architectural expression. But the crowning feature of the facade is the frieze beneath the slightly overhanging roof, which incorporates a variety of elements from Siberia's infinite wealth of ideas and the folk heritage which is always there to draw on. The application to the facade of this artistry in fretwork is evocative of the woodcarver's delicate balancing act.

La parure:
le revêtement en bois

La façade décorée

Ce qui distingue l'architecture de Tomsk de l'architecture russe ordinaire, ce sont aussi ses fascinantes suites de façades. L'architecture y met en scène une culture des fenêtres: on parcourt une rue comme on traverserait une galerie d'art. Cette architecture «joyeuse» est la rencontre de la richesse inventive, du besoin de paraître et de certaines habitudes, rencontre qui suscite une idée étonnante: la façade devenue art.

Cette idée, c'est de décorer les fenêtres et les portes, et jusqu'au toit, avec la couronne qui entoure la toiture et le bâtiment. Prenant appui sur un socle en pierre, ces façades apparaissent comme les coulisses théâtrales d'une habitation que l'on jugera à l'art de ses ouvertures: souvent doubles ou triples, les hautes fenêtres et leurs grands vitrages deviennent, par la matérialisation et la composition des détails, une entrée monumentale et couronnée, évoquant la fête. Dans ces décors en bois, on retrouve Byzance, le baroque russe, le classicisme, mais aussi l'art populaire. Les motifs en sont empruntés au monde végétal comme à la broderie, ou encore au théâtre. L'architecture se fait danse et allégresse: les bois finement ajourés mettent les maisons en habits de fête.

Les riches encadrements de cette architecture de fenêtres datent d'avant le milieu du XVIIIe siècle; à cette époque, on les trouve déjà appliqués sur les parois en rondins ou en madriers. Dans ces éléments précieux, on retrouve l'influence de Saint-Pétersbourg, alors métropole architecturale et lieu de rencontre de nombreux architectes russes et étrangers, mais aussi lieu de travail de milliers de charpentiers, de menuisiers et de maçons. C'est à un architecte italien, Bartolomeo Rastrelli (1700–1771), que l'on doit de somptueux châssis de fenêtres, promus au rôle d'éléments essentiels sur une façade dans laquelle ils apparaissent comme des coulisses: extérieurs et impressionnants, ils cachent des intérieurs plutôt modestes en général, même si une hauteur inhabituelle confère aux pièces une élégance certaine.

A Tomsk, les façades sont ordonnées selon une chorégraphie qui fait briller les fenêtres en applique comme des bijoux d'ornement. Couleur bois naturel ou diversement colorées, avec des tons pastel aussi, qu'elles soient appliquées sur la couleur du bois massif ou sur un revêtement d'une autre teinte, les fenêtres forment un contraste vertical sur l'assemblage horizontal des rondins et des madriers, tout en participant au même ouvrage d'art.

De maison en maison et à travers plusieurs quartiers, les maisons en bois sont les signes distinctifs d'un lieu et d'une histoire. Même si, aujourd'hui, leur rénovation est une nécessité urgente, les superbes bâtisses citadines autrefois réparties en échiquier dans toute l'agglomération gardent une importante valeur d'usage et une signification architecturale considérable: elles incarnent le style d'une ville tel qu'il nous est resté et tel qu'il s'était développé au cours des siècles, artistique et exceptionnel.

Une fenêtre en applique pour encadrer des images

Par le choix des couleurs et des formes, les fenêtres des maisons en bois de Tomsk et leurs compositions raffinées produisent une diversité étonnante dans le paysage, avec un effet proche du trompe-l'œil. Mais, en même temps, les reliefs en bois et leurs contours se détachent clairement du fond de façade, mêlant la subtilité de leurs lignes à la netteté du contraste. Avec sa magie ornementale, cette ancienne architecture bois est d'une beauté grandiose. Elle est exemplaire dans sa logique extrême: structure visible et volonté architecturale permettent d'en percevoir déjà de l'extérieur tout l'art de la construction.

En applique sur la façade, fenêtres et portes sont décorées, à l'image des détails ornementés que l'on trouve en dessous du toit. Parfaitement intégrés dans la composition de la façade, ces éléments amènent cependant une division de son espace et un effet de transparence. Continue et uniforme sur toute la façade, la ligne modulaire devient harmonique.

La haute fenêtre et les bois qui la partagent ainsi que le bouquet de fleurs sur son rebord limitent la perspective. Lorsqu'on regarde dehors depuis l'intérieur, dedans depuis l'extérieur, c'est une sorte de tableau que l'on contemple, dont le cadre serait la fenêtre. Vue de plus loin, celle-ci embellit la façade, comme si elle était brodée sur la surface paisible des poutres massives. Ces ouvertures relient le monde intérieur au monde extérieur. Le cadre de la fenêtre devient ainsi un élément actif de l'expression architecturale. Couronnant la composition de la façade, au-dessous du toit qui avance légèrement, la couronne de rive est un mélange et une variation à partir de l'infinie richesse de l'imagination sibérienne, qui revient sans cesse puiser dans un nouveau fonds populaire. Taillée à la scie, c'est un ouvrage d'art qui tient de la magie dans la sculpture sur bois.

Die Holzverschalung – das Verkleidende

Die dekorierte Fassade

Was Tomsk von der üblichen russischen Volksarchitektur unterscheidet, sind auch die faszinierenden Fassadenfolgen seiner Häuser. Architektur ist hier die Inszenierung einer Fensterkultur: man geht durch die Straßen wie durch eine Galerie. Diese «fröhliche» Architektur entstand aus der Verbindung von Erfindungsreichtum, Repräsentationsbedürfnis und auch Gewohnheiten zu einer überraschungsreichen Idee mit einer großen fassadenkünstlerischen Wirkung.

Diese architektonische Idee besteht im Dekorieren von Fenstern und Türen und dem um das Dach und um das Gebäude herumgeführten Kranz. Die Fassaden, die auf dem Erdgeschoß aus Stein fast wie gebaute Kulissen wirken, sind also an der Kunst ihrer Öffnungen zu «messen»: Die hohen Fenster, oft Doppel- und Dreifachfenster mit großen Scheiben, werden durch die Materialisierung und Detailgestaltung zum «gekrönten Tor», welches die Fassaden ziert, und so zum Symbol des Festlichen überhaupt. Der Stil dieses Schnitzwerkes geht zurück auf Byzanz, auf den russischen Barock, den Klassizismus und auch auf die Volkskunst. Die verwendeten Motive stammen aus der Pflanzenwelt, aber auch aus der Stickereiornamentik und aus dem Bereich des Theaters. Wahrlich eine Architektur, der das Tanzen beigebracht wurde: Die Schnitzereien, ein Lieblingsbereich des Volksschaffens, legen den Häusern das Festkleid an.

Die reichen Zargentypen dieser Fensterarchitektur wurden schon vor Mitte des 18. Jahrhunderts vor die Blockbauwand angeschlagen. Solche baukünstlerischen Kostbarkeiten gehen auf den Einfluß der damaligen Architekturmetropole zurück, auf die Stadt St. Petersburg, in der zahlreiche ausländische und russische Architekten, aber auch Tausende von russischen Zimmerleuten, Tischlern und Maurern wirkten. Der italienische Architekt Bartolomeo Rastrelli (1700–1771) hat dort prachtvolle Fenstereinfassungen zum wesentlichen Fassadenglied entwickelt. Derartige Fassadengestaltungen haben eine gewisse Kulissenhaftigkeit an sich. Die eindrucksvolle Außenfassade beherbergt nämlich im allgemeinen recht bescheidene Innenräume, obwohl die Stockwerkshöhen überdurchschnittlich waren und somit eher vornehmen Charakter hatten.

Die Fassaden in Tomsk wirken wie choreographierte Baukörper, in denen die vorgehängten Fenster als schmückende Kleinode brillieren. Im reinen Holzton, vielfach auch pastellfarbig, sind sie vor den naturfarbenen Holzblock oder vor die farbgetönte Verschalung gestellt – immer als vertikaler Kontrast zur horizontalen Gliederung durch Block oder Brett und doch zu einem Gesamtkunstwerk verknüpft.

Der Bezug auf Tomsk als Ort und auf seine Geschichte geht im Planerischen von Haus zu Haus und über mehrere Quartier-Viertel. Obwohl renovationsbedürftig, besitzen diese repräsentativen Stadthäuser, ursprünglich im Schachbrettmuster über die ganze Stadt verteilt, auch heute noch einen hohen Gebrauchswert und stellen noch immer eine große und einheitliche städtebauliche Leistung dar: Sie verkörpern den erhalten gebliebenen einzigartigen Baustil einer Stadt, der sich über Jahrhunderte in künstlerischer Einmaligkeit entwickelt hat.

Das vorgehängte Kastenfenster als Bilderrahmen

Das raffinierte Arrangement der Fenstereinheiten erzeugt bei den Holzbauten in Tomsk verschiedene Optiken in der Farb- und Formwahl: Farben und Formen vermögen so das Auge fast zu überlisten. Zugleich sind die Holzprofile der Fenster als Konturen von der Fassadenfläche klar abgehoben, und es entstehen fein verlaufende Motive mit extremer Kontrastwirkung. Die Schönheit dieser «Perle» altsibirischer Holzbaukunst mit ihrem ornamentalen Zauber wirkt überwältigend. Es ist eine exemplarische Architektur von äußerster Konsequenz: Die sichtbare Konstruktion dieser Häuser verbindet sich mit einem architektonischen Formwillen und macht die Baukunst förmlich auch von außen lesbar.

Der Fassade vorgehängt sind die dekorierten Fenster und Türen bis zu den Zierdetails unter dem Dach. Diese äußeren Bauteile passen sich optimal in die Fassadengestaltung ein. Zugleich hebt sich das Fenster von der Fassade als eine räumliche Begrenzung ab und wird so zu einem Symbol der Transparenz. Durch die einheitliche Moduldurchbildung über das ganze Gebäude ist eine harmonische Linie gegeben. So sind in Tomsk Holzhäuser mit großzügigen hohen Räumen entstanden, die auch heutigen Ansprüchen noch voll genügen.

Das hohe Fenster mit den Fensterkreuzen und dem Blumenstrauß auf dem Sims begrenzen den Ausblick. Wer von innen nach außen, aber auch von außen nach innen schaut, sieht deshalb eine Art Bild. Dieser Bildausschnitt erhält durch das Fenster seinen Rahmen. Aus größerer Entfernung betrachtet, idealisiert das Fenster mit seiner ornamentalen Einfassung aber auch die Fassadengestalt – als ob es auf die durch das Balkenmaß der Blockhäuser gegebene ruhige Holzfläche der Fassaden gestickt wäre. Diese Öffnungen setzen die innere Welt mit der äußeren in Beziehung. Der Fensterrahmen wird so zu einem Element des aktiven architektonischen Ausdrucks. Doch den krönenden Höhepunkt in der Fassadengestaltung bildet der Abschluß unter dem leicht vorstehenden Dach: als eine Mischung und Variation des unendlichen sibirischen Ideenreichtums, die bei jeder Lösung wieder auf neues Volksgut zurückgreift. Dieses auf die Fassade aufgebrachte Laubsägekunstwerk beschwört den Balanceakt der Schnitzkunst.

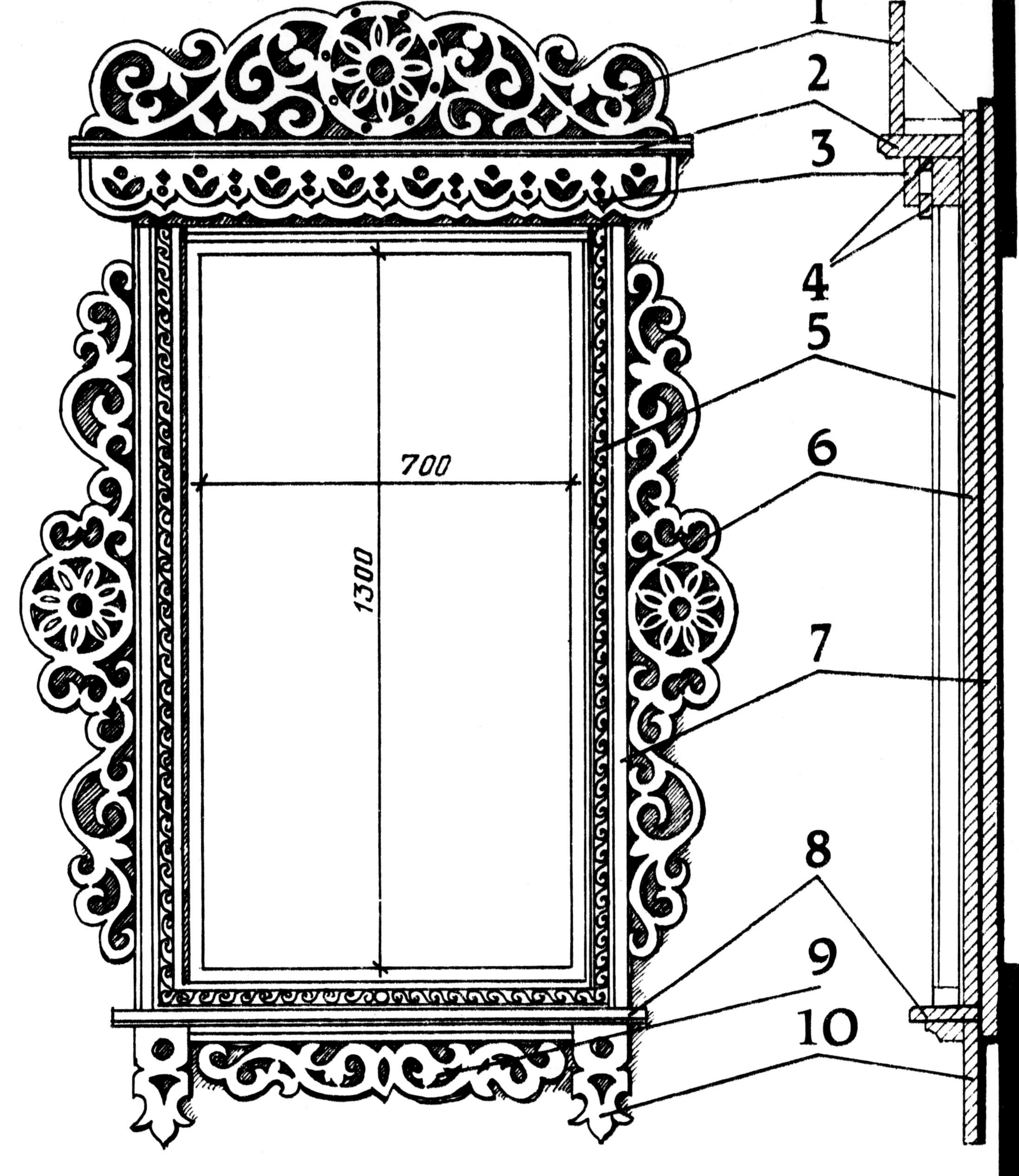

Pattern for window ornamentation
(scale 1:10).
1 Crowning element with scroll
and arabesque motifs
2 Bracket
3 Masking board
4 Supporting strips for carvings
5 Decorative mouldings
6 Lateral part of surround
7 Block frame of box window
8 Sill
9 Sill trim
10 False bracket

Composition décorative d'une
fenêtre (échelle 1:10).
1 couronnement avec volutes et
ramages
2 corbeau
3 planche de rive
4 supports de sculptures
5 baguette décorative profilée
6 encadrement de côté
7 cadre plein
8 corniche
9 baguette de corniche
10 fausse console

Vorlage für Fensterzierat
(Maßstab 1:10).
1 Bekrönung mit Voluten-,
Rankenmotiven
2 Konsole
3 Abdeckbrett
4 Unterlagenleisten für
Schnitzwerk
5 Profilierte Zierleisten
6 Seiteneinfassung
7 Blockrahmen des Kastenfensters
8 Gesims
9 Gesimszierleiste
10 Blendkonsole

From block structure to cladding.

Du rondin au revêtement.

Vom Holzblock zur Verschalung.

The window surrounds and the vertical frieze with scrolls are the product of centuries of evolution.

Les cadres de fenêtre et la frise verticale avec volutes racontent un siècle d'histoire.

Die Fenstereinfassungen und der vertikale Fries mit Voluten haben eine jahrhundertlange Entwicklungsgeschichte.

51

Dwelling house on Gagarin Street in Tomsk, with forms of the traditional Russian style of wood construction.

Habitation de la rue Gagarine à Tomsk, avec des formes traditionnelles de l'architecture bois russe.

Wohnhaus an der Gagarin Straße in Tomsk mit Formen des traditionellen russischen Holzbaustils.

The monolithic overall impression
of the houses is a result of the
cladding of the log structure. The
windows have the effect of a
counterpoint.

L'impression d'ensemble qui se
dégage de ces maisons, celle
d'unités fermées, est liée au
revêtement des façades en rondins
ou en madriers. Sur ce fond, les
fenêtres s'affirment en contrepoint.

Der geschlossene Gesamteindruck
der Häuser gründet in der
Verschalung des Blockbaus. Die
Fenster wirken dazu wie ein
Kontrapunkt.

Horizontal weatherboarding and
narrow pilasters decorated with
relief arabesques.

Revêtement de façade horizontal et
étroits pilastres, ornés d'arabesques
en relief.

Horizontale Fassadenverkleidung
und schmale, mit Reliefarabesken
verzierte Pilaster.

54

As in the wood empire of
St. Petersburg, the structural
carpentry is almost entirely hidden
behind the cladding.

Comme dans l'empire du bois de
Saint-Pétersbourg, le travail
proprement dit du charpentier est
ici presque entièrement caché
derrière le lambrissage de planches.

Wie im Holzempire von
St. Petersburg ist die eigentliche
Zimmermannsarbeit fast völlig
hinter der Brettverschalung
verborgen.

Russian Baroque and Classicism crafted in wood by local artisans.

Baroque russe et classicisme traduits en bois par les artisans locaux.

Russischer Barock und Klassizismus, von örtlichen Handwerkern in Holz gestaltet.

Palace architecture in the tradition
of Bartolomeo Rastrelli.

Architecture de palais dans la
tradition de Bartolomeo Rastrelli.

Palastarchitektur in der Tradition
Bartolomeo Rastrellis.

Shutters artistically fitted into the framework.

Volets artistiquement intégrés dans le cadre de la fenêtre.

Künstlerisch ins Rahmenwerk eingepaßte Fensterläden.

Sheathing with wooden elements
imitates stone construction.

Des éléments de revêtement en
bois imitent la construction en
pierre.

Verkleidende Holzelemente
imitieren den Steinbau.

This two-storeyed house, an artistic monument exhibiting a great wealth of forms, stands back from the street in a small garden. The octagonal, tapered ridge turrets are ornamented with carved scrolls.

Cette maison à deux étages, monument artistique aux formes d'une grande richesse, est en retrait de la rue, dans un jardin sur cour. Les clochetons octogonaux sont décorés de volutes sculptées.

Dieses zweistöckige Wohnhaus, ein künstlerisches Baudenkmal mit großem Formenreichtum, steht, von der Straße zurückgesetzt, in einem Hofgarten. Die achteckigen, kegelförmigen Dachreiter sind mit geschnitzten Voluten ausgestattet.

While the window is decorated with round Baroque forms, the gable triangle displays plant patterns.

Tandis que la fenêtre est ornée de formes rondes au style baroque, le pignon arbore des motifs végétaux.

Während das Fenster mit runden barocken Formen verziert ist, weist das Giebelfeld vegetative Muster auf.

The gables are adorned with
stylised firebirds.

Sur les pignons, des oiseaux de feu
stylisés.

An den Giebeln sind stilisierte
Feuervögel angebracht.

Both sides of the building are embellished by oriels which end under the sharply pointed triangles of the small decorative gables. The walls of the oriels are constructed as large three-sectioned windows.

Le bâtiment est agrémenté des deux côtés par des oriels qui se terminent sous les triangles pointus des petits pignons décoratifs. De grandes fenêtres en trois parties constituent les parois des oriels.

Das Gebäude wird an beiden Seiten von angebauten Erkern bereichert, die unter den scharfen Dreiecken der kleinen Ziergiebel enden. Die Erkerwände sind als große dreiteilige Fenster ausgeführt.

Mortar jointing between the logs,
with weatherboarding over it.

Joints au mortier entre les rondins
de bois, recouverts d'un
lambrissage.

Mörtelausfugung zwischen den
Holzblöcken, darüber die
Verschalung.

64

The style of this decor with its curlicues is influenced by oriental traditions (renovated).

Avec ses entrelacs, le style de ce décor (rénové) est marqué par des traditions orientales.

Der Stil dieses Dekors mit seinen Schnörkeln ist von orientalischen Traditionen geprägt (renoviert).

The beauty of the upstairs rooms
has found expression in the
arrangement of the upper parts of
the facade.

La beauté des pièces de l'étage
supérieur s'est exprimée dans la
composition des parties hautes de
la façade.

Die Schönheit der oberen
Gemächer fand ihren Ausdruck in
der Gestalt der oberen
Fassadenpartien.

A fabulously ornamented cornice
with a wooden rosette in the gable.

Une corniche de rive en couronne,
à l'ornementation fabuleusement
riche, et une rosace en bois dans le
pignon.

Ein märchenhaft reich
geschmückter Gesimskranz mit
einer Holzrosette im Giebel.

Seen from below, the narrow
gutters widen towards the cornice,
beyond which they protrude to
terminate in a pointed end.

Vues de dessous, les gouttières se
font plus larges vers la corniche,
passent par-dessus, pour se
terminer enfin en pointe.

Von unten gesehen, werden die
Abflußrinnen mit kleinem
Durchmesser zum Gesims hin
breiter, ragen darüber hinaus und
enden schließlich in einem spitzen
Abschluß.

"Lace fringes" carved from wood
are reminiscent of filigree oriental
decorative motifs.

Des «franges pointues» sculptées
dans le bois rappellent des motifs
orientaux d'ornementation en
filigrane.

Aus Holz geschnitzte
«Spitzenfransen» erinnern an
filigrane orientalische Ziermotive.

The facade detail and window
configuration exhibit a noble
simplicity.

Détail de façade et composition de
fenêtres dans une noble simplicité.

Fassadendetail und Fenstergestalt
zeigen eine noble Einfachheit.

A protective iron grille in front of
the window.

Une grille métallique protège le
cadre de la fenêtre.

Vor der Fenstereinrahmung ein
Eisengitter als Schutz.

The wooden cornice – the finishing touch

The high art of wood carving and fretwork

In the wood carvings in the traditional buildings of Tomsk, a large number of symbols developed which impart a high artistic significance to the houses. These, however, represent neither luxury nor ostentation. Every decoration has a functional meaning. The massive decorated window frames placed in front of the facade, for instance, are intended to emphasize the opening – in some cases with double windows. A decorated and protective board in the form of a pilaster is placed over the vertical, continuous join in the logs whose length is exactly measured. These pilasters are usually found in the middle of a building or as a means of finishing a corner, or as a column motif with significant symbols.

In the same way, the decorated frieze placed on the building as a finishing touch is an artistic challenge but also the product of functional needs. The various ornaments are not mere decorations, but are drawn from ideas forming part of a cultural heritage. The carved elements, mounted on the facade on thin boards, have a strong expressive force with a deep shadow effect. The simple wooden ornamentation, handed down from generation to generation, is improvised art created in the past by unknown carpenters. The tools of these wood-carvers were the axe, saw, plane and chisel. Here the work of the carpenter can almost be compared with the art of the jeweller.

The wooden houses in Tomsk are generally positioned at right angles to the street with their narrow side facing the roadway; the main entrance is on the yard side, where the oriels, galleries and staircases are located. Around the house there is generally a kitchen garden to supply the needs of the inhabitants, or a flower garden. In front of the house, in a grass border, there is often an avenue of trees running along the roadway. An aristocratic appearance is still lent to many houses by portals with original incised carvings and an architrave, often slightly curved.

Only a few of these magnificent houses whose appearance is dominated by their harmonious windows placed in front of the facade have been restored. Most of the houses that formerly belonged to the families of rich merchants are now inhabited by several families. The visitor who comes into contact with these people is impressed by their warmth and friendliness, and at the same time senses the traditional visual and inspirational sources of this folk art that are still alive today.

Bold texture

The elementary origins of log buildings are divulged by their for the most part visible structures. In the houses of Tomsk, a clear-cut timber structure is blended with the stylistic feeling of a bold, applied texture. Sometimes there is an indulgence in colours and ornamental splendour. The original character of the friezes awakens memories of the turn of the century; the noble Siberian accent of the decoration of the bargeboards and eaves is impressive as a complete unit. The whole breathes the style and character of a bygone era. These buildings could serve as a model: They invite one to stand still, to look and to reflect. And one truly does need leisure in order better to perceive and understand, for instance, the shadow lines of the ornamentations placed in front of the facade and all the beauty and outstanding talent which the carpenters of a hundred years ago put into their bold and skilful work. The massive wooden houses with their decorated facades then record history, the history of the town and of the region.

The Trans-Siberian railway brought with it economic development, creating prosperity and thus the material basis for this facade art. Furthermore, the spectacular designs for the creation of this texture in wood could never have been executed without industrialisation and the possibilities offered by power-driven sawing machines. Finally, the Siberian climate has contributed to the utility of these houses and also to their preservation. In the cold winter the wooden cubes are as if in deep freeze; during the rest of the year sun and wind ensure good ventilation. Thus Nature has done a good deal to ensure that these wooden houses in Tomsk still seem pleasant places to live in although they are in urgent need of restoration.

From the aesthetic viewpoint, the architectural heritage of Tomsk seems particularly unusual. The window, above all, is a typical feature: with its combination of functionality and imaginative forms, it takes on human proportions while at the same time conveying a feeling of spaciousness and grandeur. These wooden houses of elementary structure show imagination at play – they tread the narrow dividing line between reality and dream.

La haute école du bois ciselé à la scie

Dans la construction traditionnelle de Tomsk sont apparus un grand nombre de motifs symboliques sculptés, qui confèrent aux maisons une incontestable dimension artistique. Il ne s'agit cependant ni de luxe, ni d'ostentation. Les ornements ont aussi une fonction. Le cadre monumental de la fenêtre en applique souligne l'ouverture – souvent avec doubles fenêtres. Au joint d'assemblage vertical des bois ronds de même longueur, on trouve en général un pilastre qui est à la fois ornementation et protection. Il se répète souvent dans le milieu, ou en assemblage d'angle, ou encore en motif de colonnade, orné de symboles chargés de significations.

De même, la frise ornementale, qui est finition du bâtiment en même temps que défi artistique, répond elle aussi à des exigences fonctionnelles. Plutôt que de véritables décorations, ce sont les représentations d'un héritage culturel. Minces planches posées sur la façade, les éléments sculptés prennent une force expressive remarquable avec leurs effets d'ombre et de lumière. Transmise de génération en génération, l'ornementation simple en bois a été créée d'abord par des charpentiers inconnus, qui ont improvisé, et dont les outils étaient la hache, la scie, le rabot, le ciseau et le burin. Leur travail peut se comparer à celui d'un joaillier.

La plupart des maisons de Tomsk présentent à la rue leur côté étroit tandis que leur entrée principale se trouve côté cour. C'est là aussi que se trouvent des oriels, des galeries et des dépendances abritant les cages d'escalier. Un jardin potager ou à fleurs entoure la maison. Sur une bordure herbeuse, des arbres forment une allée devant la rue. Çà et là, des portails à l'allure aristocratique ont survécu, avec des inscriptions gravées et une architrave souvent légèrement cintrée.

De ces superbes maisons aux fenêtres en applique, imposantes et harmonieuses, rares sont celles qui ont été restaurées. Autrefois propriété de riches commerçants, elles sont aujourd'hui partagées entre plusieurs familles. De la rencontre avec ces gens, il reste le sentiment d'une grande gentillesse et d'une proximité vécue avec des sources d'inspiration visuelles et des traditions poétiques encore vivaces de l'art populaire.

Audacieuse texture

Les structures, le plus souvent apparentes, de la construction en rondins ou en madriers trahissent leurs origines élémentaires. C'est le mélange d'un bâti bois clairement affirmé avec la sensibilité esthétique d'une audacieuse texture en applique. Parfois, on se grise de couleurs et d'ornementations précieuses. Les couronnes de finition évoquent le début du siècle; le noble accent sibérien des ornementations de larmier et de bordure de pignon est impressionnant. Il s'en dégage le parfum subtil d'une époque surannée. Ces bâtiments sont exemplaires: ils invitent à s'arrêter, à regarder, à réfléchir. Et il faut en effet prendre du temps pour mieux percevoir et mieux comprendre les lignes d'ombre des décors en applique, toute la beauté et toute la valeur du savoirfaire et de l'audace que des charpentiers d'il y a cent ans ont mis en œuvre dans ces ouvrages. Les formidables maisons en bois, avec leur parure de façade, racontent alors l'histoire, celle du lieu et de la région.

Le chemin de fer transsibérien a apporté le développement économique, c'est-à-dire la prospérité qui a permis matériellement cet art des façades. Mais sans les possibilités nouvelles offertes par l'industrialisation et ses scies mécaniques, il eût été également impensable de réaliser ces extraordinaires textures en bois. Enfin, c'est au climat sibérien que l'on doit d'avoir conservé ces maisons et de pouvoir encore les habiter. Pendant les grands froids, les cubes en bois sont comme congelés; le reste de l'année, soleil et vent les tempèrent et les aèrent. La nature a donc mis du sien pour que les maisons en bois de Tomsk continuent à être accueillantes et habitables, même si elles ont terriblement besoin d'être restaurées.

C'est d'un point de vue esthétique plus particulièrement que l'héritage architectonique de Tomsk sort de l'ordinaire. La fenêtre surtout est typique: parfaitement adaptée à sa fonction, elle déborde d'imagination dans ses formes et, prenant proportions humaines, elle devient monumentale et généreuse. Ces élémentaires maisons en bois sont un jeu de l'imagination – elles se meuvent sur l'étroite frange qui sépare la réalité du rêve.

Der Holzkranz – das Abschließende

Die hohe Schule der Schnitz- und Sägekunst

In der Tradition des Tomsker Bauens entstanden am Schnitzwerk eine Vielzahl von Symbolen, die den Häusern eine große künstlerische Bedeutung geben. Aber es handelt sich weder um Luxus noch um Prunk. Jede Zierde hat ihre funktionelle Bedeutung. Der gewaltige, vorgesetzte Fensterrahmen mit Zierschmuck etwa will die Öffnung – zum Teil mit Doppelfenster – hervorheben. Über die vertikale, durchgehende Fuge der in der Länge abgemessenen Rundhölzer ist eine verzierte und schützende Brettlisene angebracht. Meistens finden wir sie in der Mitte oder auch als Ecklösung eines Bauwerks oder als Säulenmotiv mit signifikanten Zeichen.

So ist auch der geschmückte, aufgesetzte Fries als Gebäudeabschluß eine künstlerische Herausforderung und zugleich doch aus funktionellen Forderungen entstanden. Es sind darum nicht eigentliche Dekorationen, sondern Ideen eines kulturellen Erbes. Die Schnitzelemente, die in dünnen Brettern auf der Fassade aufliegen, erhalten eine markante Ausdruckskraft mit einer tiefen Schattenwirkung. Der einfache Holzschmuck, von Generation zu Generation überliefert, wurde von unbekannten Zimmerleuten als Improvisationskunst geschaffen. Die Werkzeuge dieser Holzschnitzer waren Beil, Säge, Hobel, Stechbeitel und Meissel. Fast könnte man sagen, diese Zimmermannsarbeiten sind mit der Juwelierkunst vergleichbar.

Im allgemeinen sind die Holzhäuser in Tomsk mit der Schmalseite gegen die Straße quer gestellt; der Haupteingang findet sich an der Hofseite. Dort sind auch Erker, Galerien und Anbauten für Treppenhäuser. Um das Haus herum ist meist ein Gemüsegarten zur Selbstversorgung oder ein Blumengarten angelegt. Vor dem Haus findet sich vielfach in einer Grasrabatte die Baumallee, an der die Verkehrsstraße vorbeiführt. Verschiedentlich bestehen heute noch aristokratisch anmutende Portale mit originell eingravierten Schnitzereien und einem Architrav, oft in leicht gebogener Form.

Nur wenige dieser stattlichen Häuser mit den dominierenden, vorgesetzten harmonischen Fenstern sind restauriert. Die meisten Häuser, die früher reichen Kaufmannsfamilien gehörten, werden heute von mehreren Familien bewohnt. Die Begegnungen mit diesen Menschen lassen den Besucher eine große Liebenswürdigkeit erfahren und zugleich die noch immer lebendigen visuellen Inspirationsquellen und musischen Traditionen dieser Volkskunst spüren.

Kühne Textur

Die mehrheitlich sichtbaren Konstruktionen des Blockbaus verraten ihren elementaren Ursprung. Es ist die Vermischung eines klaren Holzgefüges mit dem Stilgefühl einer aufgesetzten, kühnen Textur. Zum Teil wird in Farben und kostbaren Verzierungen geschwelgt. Die originellen Dachkränze rufen die Erinnerung an die Jahrhundertwende wach; der noble sibirische Akzent der Wind- und Stirnbrettverzierung ist als Ganzheit beeindruckend. Alles atmet den stilvollen Charakter einer vergangenen Zeit. Diese Bauten könnten Vorbild sein: Sie verleiten zum Stehenbleiben, Schauen und Nachdenken. Und es braucht in der Tat Muße, um etwa die Schattenlinien der vorgesetzten Zierelemente und all das Schöne und Beachtenswerte, das die damaligen Zimmerleute vor hundert Jahren an Können und Kühnheit ins Werk gesetzt haben, besser wahrzunehmen und zu verstehen. Die mächtigen Holzhäuser mit ihrem Fassadenschmuck erzählen dann Geschichte, die Geschichte des Ortes und der Region.

Die transsibirische Eisenbahn brachte wirtschaftlichen Aufschwung, damit Wohlstand und so die materielle Grundlage für diese Fassadenkunst. Ohne die Möglichkeit, welche die Industrialisierung mit den mechanisch betriebenen Sägemaschinen bot, wären die sensationellen Lösungen zur Verwirklichung dieser Textur in Holz wohl ebensowenig realisierbar gewesen. Zur Brauchbarkeit und auch zur Erhaltung dieser Häuser trug schließlich das sibirische Klima bei. Im kalten Winter sind die Holzkuben wie eingefroren; in den übrigen Jahreszeiten sorgen Sonne und Wind für eine gute Durchlüftung. Die Natur hat also durchaus das Ihre getan, daß diese Holzhäuser in Tomsk noch immer freundlich und bewohnbar wirken, obwohl sie dringend restaurationsbedürftig sind.

Das architektonische Erbe von Tomsk erscheint besonders unter ästhetischem Gesichtspunkt ungewöhnlich. Typisch ist vor allem das Fenster: zweckmäßig in seiner Funktion und phantasievoll in seinen Formen, nimmt es die menschlichen Proportionen auf und wirkt zugleich ebenso großzügig wie großartig. So sind diese elementaren Holzhäuser ein klares Spiel der Phantasie – sie bewegen sich auf dem schmalen Grat zwischen Wirklichkeit und Traum.

There is a wide range of window
designs: from the modest board
decorated with simple geometrical
carvings to complex ornamentation.

Dans la composition des fenêtres,
l'éventail est vaste: de la modeste
planche ornée d'une simple
sculpture géométrique à
l'ornementation compliquée.

Das Spektrum für die Gestaltung
der Fenster ist weit: vom
bescheidenen, mit einfacher
geometrischer Schnitzerei
verzierten Brett bis zur
komplizierten Ornamentik.

Wood carving is an art of improvisation kindred to that of the jeweller.

La sculpture sur bois devient ici un art de l'improvisation qui se rapproche de celui du joaillier.

Holzschnitzerei als eine Improvisationskunst, die der Juwelierkunst nahesteht.

76

The decor as fancy dress – such carvings are often inspired by old Russian legends and folk songs.

Le décor est un habit de fête – souvent, les sculptures de ce genre trouvent aussi leur inspiration dans de vieilles légendes russes ou dans des chants populaires.

Das Dekor als Festkleid – oft sind solche Schnitzereien auch von altrussischen Sagen und Volksliedern inspiriert.

Window surround rich in variation, with plant themes as ornamentation.

Riches variations dans les encadrements de fenêtre avec leurs ornements de plantes.

Variationsreiche Fenstereinrahmung mit Pflanzenornamenten.

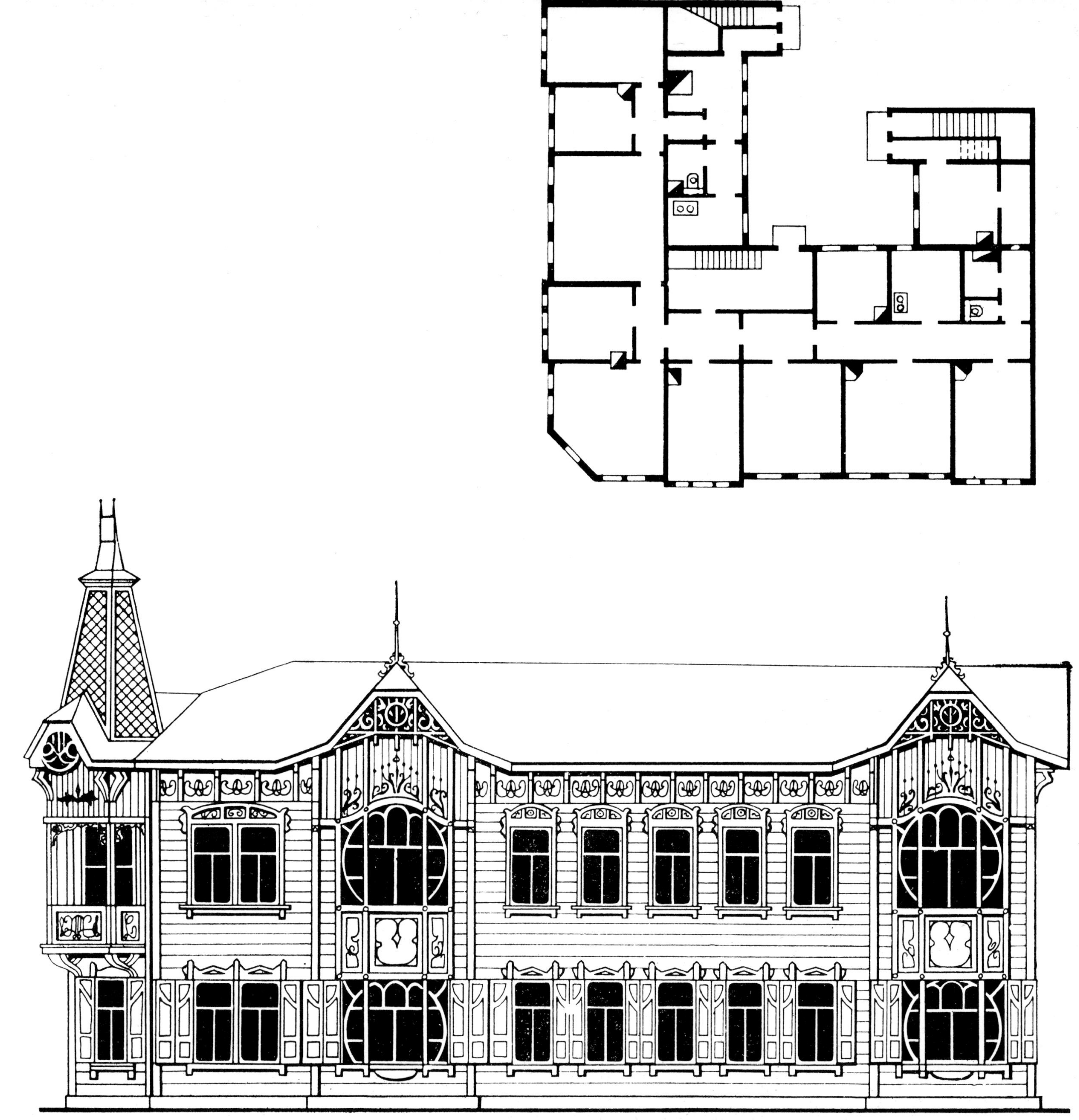

Dwelling house (built 1908) in the
Tomsk style: elevation and plan.

Habitation (construite en 1908)
dans le style de Tomsk: vue en
élévation et en plan.

Wohnhaus im Tomsker Stil (erbaut
1908): Ansicht und Grundriß.

Window surrounds and cornice brackets with motifs from oriental embroidery and carpets.

Encadrements de fenêtre et corbeaux de corniche, avec des motifs que l'on retrouve dans les broderies et les tapis d'Orient.

Fenstereinrahmungen und Simskonsolen mit Motiven wie auf orientalischen Stickereien und Teppichen.

The houses in Tomsk feature
practically divisioned, large-paned
windows.

Les maisons de Tomsk possèdent
de grandes fenêtres à carreaux.

Die Häuser in Tomsk besitzen
großflächige Fenster mit
praktischer Einteilung.

Curious contrast effects are
produced by the light and dark
tones of the block structure and the
palace-like style of the window
distribution.

Le clair-obscur du rondin en bois et
la distribution des fenêtres digne
d'un palais forment des contrastes
saisissants.

Das Hell-Dunkel des Holzblocks
und der palastartige Stil der
Fenstereinteilung lassen
eigenartige Kontraste entstehen.

The high rooms of the Tomsk
dwelling houses give the windows
a slender and at the same time
monumental appearance.

Parce que les pièces, dans les
maisons de Tomsk, sont hautes, les
fenêtres apparaissent à la fois
élancées et monumentales.

Die große Raumhöhe der Tomsker
Wohnhäuser macht die Fenster
schlank und monumental zugleich.

This wood carving in the Baroque and Classicistic styles imitates old Russian lace and embroidery; it is also adorned with stylised plant ornaments and carved spiral columns.

Cette sculpture en bois alliant style baroque et style classique imite les anciennes dentelles et broderies russes; elle est, de plus, décorée de plantes stylisées et de colonnes sculptées et spiralées.

Diese Holzschnitzerei im Stil des Barocks und des Klassizismus ahmt altrussische Spitzen und Stickereien nach; sie ist außerdem mit stilisierten Pflanzenornamenten sowie geschnitzten und gewundenen Säulen verziert.

Windows placed close to each other
with slender pilasters demonstrate
Classical forms and a rectilinear
configuration, combined with rich
decoration.

Des fenêtres en alignement
compact avec d'étroits pilastres
expriment la forme et la linéarité
classiques, alliées à une riche
ornementation.

Dicht aneinandergeordnete Fenster
mit engen Lisenen demonstrieren
klassische Form und
Geradlinigkeit, verbunden mit
reichem Zierwerk.

House at Shishkov Street 14.

Maison de la rue Chichkov 14.

Haus an der Schischkow Straße 14.

Richly decorated window units positioned close to each other make the houses appear taller and more slender than they really are.

Richement décorées et très proches les unes des autres, les fenêtres font paraître les maisons plus hautes et plus élancées qu'elles ne le sont.

Reich verzierte, eng aneinanderliegende Fenstereinheiten lassen die Häuser höher und schlanker erscheinen, als sie sind.

The widely projecting eaves
mouldings are combined with
ornamental brackets.

Corniches, corbeaux ouvragés et
couronnes de toiture formant un
large encorbellement.

Die Gesimse weisen verzierte
Konsolen mit weitauskragenden
Dachkränzen auf.

88–91
Palace-like houses at Shishkov
Street in Tomsk.

A la rue Chichkov, à Tomsk, des
maisons aux allures de palais.

Palastartige Häuser an der
Schischkow Straße in Tomsk.

The writer Viacheslav Yakovlevich
Shishkov lived at Shishkov Street
No. 10 (1911–1915). The building
stands on a stone base; the cornice
line under the roof projects far
forward and is supported by carved
brackets.

C'est ici, au numéro 10, qu'a vécu
de 1911 à 1915 l'écrivain
Viatcheslav Iakovlevitch Chichkov.
Le bâtiment repose sur un socle de
pierre; la ligne de la corniche, sous
le toit, forme une large avancée et
repose sur des corbeaux sculptés.

In der Schischkow Straße wohnte
1911–1915 der Schriftsteller
Wjatscheslaw Jakowlewitsch
Schischkow. Das Gebäude ruht auf
einem Steinsockel; die Simslinie
unter dem Dach steht weit vor und
ist durch geschnitzte Konsolen
gestützt.

The whole front side of this house
is framed with narrow pilasters.
The cornice and window surrounds
are as if cast in the same mould.

Tout le devant de cette maison est
encadré par d'étroits pilastres.
Corniches et cadres de fenêtre se
fondent dans un même moule.

Die ganze Vorderseite dieses
Hauses ist mit schmalen Pilastern
eingerahmt. Sims und
Fenstereinrahmungen sind wie aus
einem Guß.

Slender pilasters with arabesques
and vignettes in the style of Russian
Classicism.

De minces pilastres avec
arabesques et vignettes dans le
style russe classique.

Schlanke Pilaster mit Arabesken
und Vignetten im Stil des
russischen Klassizismus.

90

Classical cornice, rhythmically
interrupted by a number of
ornamental gables.

Corniche classique, rythmiquement
ponctuée par plusieurs pignons
décoratifs.

Klassisches Gesims, rhythmisch
durchschnitten von mehreren
Ziergiebeln.

Decor with applied floral
ornamentation.

Décor d'ornements végétaux en
applique.

Dekor mit aufgelegten
Pflanzenornamenten.

Gate with double door and two side entrances. The high relief on the pilasters decorated with capitals and rosettes.

Portail monumental avec porte à deux vantaux et deux entrées latérales: le haut-relief sur pilastres est décoré de chapiteaux et de rosaces.

Tor mit zweiflügeliger Tür und zwei Seiteneingängen: Das Hochrelief auf den Pilastern ist mit Kapitellen und Rosetten geschmückt.

94–95
A house in the yard, flanked by
trees.

La maison se trouve dans la cour,
avec des arbres de chaque côté.

Ein Haus im Hof, von Bäumen
flankiert.

The wood cladding is framed with
comb-like ornamention.

Les bords du lambrissage en bois
sont marqués d'éléments décoratifs.

Die Holzverschalung ist mit
Zierkämmen eingefaßt.

The addition of window units
results in a frame "composition"
which extends over the whole
façade, creating the effect of
smooth "knitted" texture.

La juxtaposition des fenêtres donne
un quadrillage de la façade qui
évoque le travail patient de la
maille à travers le tricot.

Die Addition von Fenstereinheiten
ergibt ein Rahmenwerk, das sich
über die ganze Fassade erstreckt
und wie eine ruhige, «gestrickte»
Textur wirkt.

House at Belinsky Street 19 in Tomsk.

Maison de la rue Belinski 19, à Tomsk.

Haus an der Belinsky Straße 19 in Tomsk.

The steep upper corners of the gables are elements in the façade composition and at the same time set their mark on the silhouette of the building.

Formant des angles abrupts à leur extrémité supérieure, des pignons entrent dans la composition de façade en même temps qu'ils marquent la silhouette du bâtiment.

Steile Giebeloberecken sind Kompositionsteile der Fassade und prägen zugleich die Gebäudesilhouette.

The high artistic achievement of
the Tomsk carpenters can be seen
in this facade composition with its
many gables.

L'art consommé des charpentiers
de Tomsk se révèle dans cette
composition de façade avec ses
nombreux pignons.

Die hohe Kunst der Tomsker
Zimmerleute zeigt sich in dieser
Fassadenkomposition mit ihren
zahlreichen Giebeln.

98–99
Two-storeyed dwelling house.

Maison à deux étages.

Zweistöckiges Wohnhaus.

The ground floor serves as a stone wall base.

Le rez-de-chaussée, en pierre, sert de socle.

Das Parterre dient als Sockel und ist aus Stein gemauert.

Annexes such as oriels, loggias and galleries are placed on the side facing the yard.

Oriels, loggias et galeries se trouvent côté cour.

Anbauten wie Erker, Loggien und Galerien sind zum Hof ausgerichtet.

Map of Russia, scale 1:15,000,000:
Tomsk.

Carte de la Russie à l'échelle
1:15 000 000: Tomsk.

Karte von Rußland im Maßstab
1:15'000'000: Tomsk.

Detail of the present town plan of Tomsk.

Extrait d'un plan actual de la ville de Tomsk aujourd'hui.

Ausschnitt aus dem heutigen Stadtplan von Tomsk.

Larisa Stepanovna
Romanova:
Preserving the wood
architecture of Tomsk

In the year 2004 the town of Tomsk in Siberia will be four hundred years old. One of the few Russian towns that still retains much of its original character, it possesses historical districts consisting mainly of wooden buildings. Dating from the late 19th and early 20th centuries, these differ substantially from the Classicistic architecture that preceded them. Their windows are larger and the unclad surface of the log structures provides a good background for the decor which has now become a central element in the architecture of the buildings. Window surrounds, tympanums, pilasters and other details are richly ornamented with applications of fretwork and three-dimensional blind and open carvings.

The merchants, who constituted the most prosperous social class, vied with each other in building residences ever more lavish in their ornamentation. Many of these houses were constructed according to designs by the Tomsk architects K.K. Lygin, P.P. Fedorenko, W.F. Orsheshko, and by other graduates of the Imperial Academy of Arts. In the decoration of the facades they used ornaments typical of the region (geometrical motifs) and also drew upon oriental tradition (applied cartouches, fretworked tympanums). Thus a new Tomsk architecture developed based on traditional elements.

The architects' ideas were executed by simple craftsmen. The buildings are characterised by their quality and lovingly created details. The play of light and shade and the pastel tones of the oil paints applied to the details give the houses a prim and at the same time festive character. And although their present appearance is a far cry from what it formerly was, even today these houses are a heart-warming feast for the eyes. One can only be amazed by the variety and originality of their details and the fantasy and masterly skill of their creators.

With the aim of preserving this cultural legacy, the special workshop "Tomskrestavratsia", which is concerned mainly with scientific aspects and production arrangements (Director: P.S. Sukhoteply) and the Siberian branch of the "Spezproiektrestavratsia" Institute (Director: A.N. Chernov) were established in Tomsk. The latter institute produces scientific documentation on the restoration and utilisation of historical and architectural monuments. For the historical part of the town, a project for preservation zones (by the "Spezproiektrestavratsia" Institute, Moscow) and a project for the reconstruction of the town centre (by the Siberian branch of the Institute "Spezproiektrestavratsia") have been drawn up.

In view of its rich cultural heritage, in 1990 Tomsk was awarded the status of an "Historical Town". In 1992 the undertaking "Historical Tomsk" was established under the sponsorship of the town to coordinate the tackling of the problems involved in the work of preservation.

The buildings that have been restored as architectural monuments in wood include the houses at Krasnoarmeiskaya Street 68 and at Kirov Prospekt 7 (designed by the architect Kriatshkov). I was fortunate enough to be able to draw up the plans for the restoration of these wonderful "Art Nouveau" buildings and, as architect, to supervise the execution of the work. The two-storeyed house at Krasnoarmeiskaya Street 68 (formerly Soldatskaya Street) was built at the beginning of the 20th century as a dwelling house according to the plans of K.K. Lygin. It was very severely damaged by a fire in 1977. This house, which is unique in Tomsk, is reminiscent of Scandinavian architecture and is remarkable for the high quality of its construction.

The stylised dragons and the gable details have now been restored by means of templates. These were created from remnants of details and from photographs taken before the restoration. The canopy over the main entrance was reconstructed on the basis of measurements of the timber joints and drawings by K.K. Lygin that were found on a sketch in the archive, the identical decor on the roof turret being taken as a pattern for the ornamentation. The house was painted in the colour tone found in the eye of the dragon. After its restoration, this historical building was used to house an outpatient clinic, the engineer A.W. Resnikov being responsible for the plans. The work of restoration was carried out between 1978 and 1982 by the undertaking "Tomskrestavratsia".

The former villa of the engineer A.D. Kriatshkov was built in 1910 according to his own plans. The restoration project set out to restore the facades to their original appearance on the basis of photographs preserved in the archive, studies of the exterior of the building and the plans of A.D. Kriatshov. After the fire of 1982, the work on the project was conducted by the architect J.I. Bardichev and the designer S.F. Shatov.

The restoration work was done between 1981 and 1985 by the undertaking "Tomskrestavratsia". This architectural monument now houses an office.

Preservation orders now apply to 1697 objects (including archaeological monuments). Most of the architectural monuments are in wood. It is an alarming fact that most of the plans for their restoration, although ready for execution, cannot be put into effect due to a lack of funds. As a result, the plans are now outdated, the buildings are falling into decay and some of them will be irretrievably lost.

Conserver l'architecture bois de Tomsk

En 2004, la ville de Tomsk, en Sibérie, aura 400 ans. C'est une des rares villes de Russie qui ait conservé intacte l'empreinte de ses origines. Les quartiers qui témoignent aujourd'hui de son histoire abritent principalement des constructions en bois datant de la fin du XIXe et du début du XXe siècle. Ces bâtiments sont fondamentalement différents de ceux de la période classique qui les a précédés. Leurs fenêtres sont plus grandes et leur surface en rondins ou en madriers se fait support pour un décor qui commence à tenir le premier rôle dans l'architecture. Châssis de fenêtre, remplissage de pignon, pilastres et autres détails sont richement ornés de sculptures: découpées à la scie, en applique et en relief, celles-ci forment des motifs en trois dimensions, d'autant plus irréels qu'ils sont plus ajourés.

A l'époque de la construction de ces bâtiments, ce sont les commerçants qui formaient, à Tomsk, la classe sociale la plus aisée. Rivalisant dans l'expression visible de leur prospérité, ils se construisirent des maisons toutes plus ornementées les unes que les autres. Beaucoup d'entre elles ont été bâties d'après les plans d'architectes qui travaillaient à Tomsk même – K.K. Lygin, P.P. Fedorenko ou V.F. Orzheshko –, ou qui sortaient de l'Académie impériale des beaux-arts. Les décors de leurs façades s'inspirent d'ornements courants dans la région (motifs géométriques) ou empruntés aux traditions orientales (cartouches ornementaux et tympans ajourés). Dans l'architecture de Tomsk, un style de construction nouveau est ainsi né, à partir d'éléments traditionnels.

Ce sont de simples artisans qui réalisaient les idées des architectes. Leurs constructions sont donc marquées par le souci de la qualité et l'amour du détail. Par le jeu des ombres et des lumières, par les tons clairs qui font ressortir les détails peints à l'huile, les maisons se mettent en parure de fête. Aujourd'hui encore, quand on les regarde, et même si elles sont loin d'être restées ce qu'elles étaient à l'origine, on éprouve plaisir des yeux et chaud au cœur. Très diverses et uniques dans leurs détails, elles nous étonnent par l'imagination et la maîtrise qu'elles attestent chez leurs créateurs.

Afin de conserver cet héritage culturel, un atelier scientifique spécialisé a été créé à Tomsk, sous le nom de Tomskrestawrazia; dirigé par P. Suchoteply, il intervient directement sur les bâtiments. D'autre part, une filiale sibérienne de l'Institut Spezprojektrestawrazia, dirigée par A.M. Tchernov, fournit quant à elle la documentation scientifique nécessaire aux restaurations et aux affectations des monuments historiques et architecturaux.

En outre, deux projets sont en cours: l'un concerne des zones de monuments protégés dans les quartiers historiques de la ville, l'autre la reconstruction du centre ville; ils sont menés respectivement par l'Institut Spezprojektrestawrazia de Moscou et par la filiale sibérienne du même institut.

Etant donné ce riche héritage culturel, Tomsk jouit depuis 1990 du statut de ville historique. Sous le nom de «Tomsk historique», une institution a été fondée par la ville en 1992, afin de coordonner et de résoudre les différents problèmes liés au maintien de cet héritage.

Parmi les objets restaurés figurent les monuments d'architecture bois de la rue Krasnoarmeïskaia 68 et de la perspective Kirov 7 (maison dessinée par l'architecte A.D. Kriatchov). J'ai eu la chance de tracer les plans de restauration de ces superbes bâtisses qui portent l'empreinte du style Art Nouveau et d'en surveiller les travaux en ma qualité d'architecte.

La maison à deux étages de la rue Krasnoarmeïskaia 68 (jadis rue Soldatskaia) a été construite au début du XXe siècle, d'après des plans de K.K. Lygin. Lors d'un incendie, en 1977, elle a subi de gros dommages. Unique à Tomsk, cette habitation rappelle l'architecture scandinave et témoigne d'une grande recherche de qualité dans la construction.

A l'aide de gabarits confectionnés sur la base de fragments de détails conservés et de photographies prises avant la restauration, on a reconstruit les dragons stylisés et les détails du pignon. De même, l'auvent qui surmonte l'entrée principale a été refait d'après des relevés d'assemblages et des dessins de K.K. Lygin conservés dans les archives et en reprenant le décor de la tourelle du toit. Pour les façades, on a utilisé le coloris retrouvé dans l'œil des dragons. Depuis qu'il a été restauré, ce bâtiment abrite une policlinique, dont les plans ont été dessinés par l'ingénieur A.W. Reshikov. C'est Tomskrestawrazia dont nous avons parlé plus haut qui a effectué les travaux de restauration, entre 1978 et 1982.

La maison qu'occupait autrefois A.D. Kriatchov a été construite en 1910 selon les propres plans de l'architecte. Grâce à des documents photographiques conservés dans les archives, aux plans de A.D. Kriatchov et à diverses recherches, on a pu redonner à ses façades leur aspect d'origine. Après l'incendie de 1982, les travaux nécessaires ont été confiés à l'architecte J.I. Bardytchev et à l'ingénieur S.F. Schatov et exécutés par Tomskrestawrazia, entre 1981 et 1985. Aujourd'hui, la maison est occupée par des bureaux.

Actuellement, 1697 objets (et parmi eux des monuments archéologiques aussi) sont placés sous la sauvegarde de la Conservation des monuments. La plupart d'entre eux sont construits en bois. Alors que des plans existent pour leur restauration, il est alarmant de constater que, faute de moyens financiers, ils ne se réalisent pas. Peu à peu, ils deviennent dépassés, les bâtiments se délabrent et quelques-uns même sont d'ores et déjà irrémédiablement perdus.

Die Erhaltung der Holzarchitektur von Tomsk

Die sibirische Stadt Tomsk wird im Jahre 2004 vierhundert Jahre alt. Sie ist eine der wenigen Städte Rußlands, deren ursprüngliche Prägung erhalten geblieben ist. Die noch existierenden historischen Quartiere bestehen hauptsächlich aus Holzbauten vom Ende des 19. Jahrhunderts und vom Anfang des 20. Jahrhunderts. Sie unterscheiden sich wesentlich von der vorhergehenden klassizistischen Architektur. Die Fenster sind größer, und die nicht verkleidete Blockbauoberfläche bildet einen guten Hintergrund für das Dekor, das in der Architektur des Gebäudes die Hauptrolle zu spielen beginnt. Fenstereinfassungen, Giebelfüllungen, Pilaster und andere Details werden reich mit Schnitzerei verziert: mit aufgelegtem, durchgeschnittenem und ausgesägtem, mit dreidimensionalem, mit blindem und durchbrochenem Schnitzwerk.

Die wohlhabendste Gesellschaftsschicht waren die Kaufleute. In ihrem Wunsch, einander zu übertrumpfen, bauten sie Wohnhäuser, von denen eines verschnörkelter war als das andere. Viele von ihnen wurden nach Plänen der in Tomsk arbeitenden Architekten K.K. Lygin, P.P. Fedorenko, W.F. Orscheschko und anderer Absolventen der Kaiserlichen Akademie der Künste gebaut. Bei der dekorativen Gestaltung der Fassaden griffen sie auf in der Region verbreitete Ornamente (geometrische Motive) und östliche Traditionen (Auflagekartuschen, durchbrochene Tympanonfüllungen) zurück. So entstand ein aus traditionellen Elementen bestehender, für die Tomsker Architektur neuer Baustil.

Die Ideen der Architekten wurden von einfachen Handwerkern ausgeführt. Die Bauten zeichneten sich durch Qualität und liebevoll gestaltete Details aus. Das Licht-Schatten-Spiel, die hellen Töne, in denen die mit Ölfarben gestrichenen Details gehalten waren, verliehen den Häusern einen schmucken, feierlichen Charakter. Und obwohl die Häuser bei weitem nicht mehr ihre ursprüngliche Gestalt haben, sind sie noch heute eine Augenweide, und bei ihrem Anblick wird einem warm ums Herz. Sie überraschen durch die Mannigfaltigkeit und die Einmaligkeit der Details, durch die Phantasie und die Meisterschaft ihrer Schöpfer.

Um dieses historische Kulturerbe zu erhalten, wurden in Tomsk die Spezialwerkstatt «Tomskrestawrazia» mit wissenschaftlicher und produktionsbezogener Ausrichtung (Direktor: P.S. Suchoteply) und die sibirische Filiale des Instituts «Spezprojektrestawrazia» (Direktor: A.N. Tschernow) begründet. Das Institut leistet die wissenschaftliche Dokumentation über die Restaurierung und Nutzung der historischen und architektonischen Denkmäler.

Für den historischen Stadtteil wurden ein Projekt von Denkmalschutzzonen (vom Institut «Spezprojektrestawrazia», Moskau) und ein Projekt zur Rekonstruktion der Stadtmitte (von der sibirischen Filiale des Instituts «Spezprojektrestawrazia») ausgearbeitet.

In Anbetracht des reichen Kulturerbes wurde der Stadt Tomsk 1990 der Status «Historische Stadt» verliehen. Um die mit der Erhaltung des Erbes zusammenhängenden Probleme koordinieren und lösen zu können, wurde 1992 das von der Stadt getragene Unternehmen «Das historische Tomsk» gegründet.

Zu den restaurierten Objekten gehören die Holzarchitekturdenkmäler in der Krasnoarmejskaja-Str. 68 und am Kirow-Prospekt 7 (von dem Architekten Krjatschkow entworfenes Haus). Ich hatte das Glück, die Pläne für die Restaurierung dieser wunderbaren Tomsker Jugendstilholzbauten erstellen zu können und als Architektin die Renovierungsarbeiten zu überwachen.

Das zweistöckige Haus in der Krasnoarmejskaja-Str. 68 (ehemalige Soldatskaja-Straße) war Anfang des 20. Jahrhunderts nach den Plänen von K.K. Lygin als Wohnhaus gebaut worden. Bei einem Brand im Jahre 1977 wurde das Haus sehr stark beschädigt. Dieses für Tomsk einmalige Haus erinnert an skandinavische Architektur und zeichnet sich durch die hohe Qualität der Bauarbeiten aus.

Die stilisierten Drachen und die Giebeldetails wurden jetzt mit Hilfe von Schablonen wiederhergestellt. Diese wurden nach den erhalten gebliebenen Resten von Details und nach Photographien gefertigt, die vor der Restaurierung aufgenommen worden waren. Das Vordach über dem Haupteingang wurde nach Maßaufnahmen der Holzverbindungen und den Zeichnungen von K.K. Lygin wiederhergestellt, die auf einer Skizze im Archiv gefunden worden waren, und nach dem gleichen Dekor auf dem Dachtürmchen. Die Oberflächenbehandlung des Hauses wurde in dem Farbton ausgeführt, den man im Auge des Drachens gefunden hatte. Nach der Restaurierung des Denkmals wurde hier eine Poliklinik untergebracht. Der Plan dafür stammt von dem Ingenieur A.W. Resnikow. Die Restaurierungsarbeiten wurden in den Jahren 1978 – 1982 von dem Unternehmen «Tomskrestawrazia» durchgeführt.

Die ehemalige Villa des Ingenieurs A.D. Krjatschkow war im Jahre 1910 nach seinen eigenen Plänen gebaut worden. In den Restaurierungsplänen sollten die Fassaden nach den im Archiv erhalten gebliebenen Photodokumenten, nach Außenuntersuchungen und nach den Plänen von A.D. Krjatschkow wieder die ursprüngliche Gestalt bekommen. Nach dem Brand von 1982 wurden die Arbeiten an dem Projekt von dem Architekten J.I. Bardytschew und dem Konstrukteur S.F. Schatow durchgeführt.

Die Restaurierungsarbeiten wurden 1981 bis 1985 durch das Unternehmen «Tomskrestawrazia» ausgeführt. Nun befindet sich in diesem Architekturdenkmal ein Büro.

Unter Denkmalschutz stehen gegenwärtig 1697 Objekte (darunter auch archäologische Denkmäler). Die meisten der Architekturdenkmäler sind aus Holz. Es ist alarmierend, daß wegen der fehlenden Geldmittel der größte Teil der fertig vorliegenden Pläne zur Restaurierung der Denkmäler nicht ausgeführt worden ist. Infolgedessen sind die Pläne inzwischen überholt, die Gebäude werden baufällig, und einige gehen unwiederbringlich verloren.

Старинный сибирский город Томск в 2004 году будет праздновать своё 400-летие.

Томск — один из немногих городов России, сохранивший своё лицо. Существующая историческая застройка, в основном, состоит из деревянных строений конца 19го начала 20го веков и значительно отличается от предшествующей классицистической архитектуры. Увеличиваются в размерах окна, не обшитая поверхность сруба служит хорошим фоном для декора, роль которого становится главенствующей в архитектуре здания. Наличники, заполнения фронтонов, пилястры и другие детали обильно украшаются резьбой: накладной, прорезной и пропильной, объёмной, глухой и ажурной.

Наиболее состоятельным слоем общества было купечество. Состязаясь друг с другом, купцы возводили терема — один затейливее другого. Многие из них строились по проектам архитекторов, работавших в Томске — Лыгина К.К., Фёдоровского П.П., Оржешко В.Ф и других выпускников Императорской Академии Художеств. В декоративном оформлении фасадов архитекторы использовали местные орнаменты (геометрические мотивы), восточные традиции (накладные картуши, восточные ажурные заполнения тимпанов). Так создавался традиционный стиль, новый для томской архитектуры.

Замыслы архитекторов воплощали народные умельцы. Постройки отличались добротностью, любовно выполненными деталями. Игра света и тени, светлые колера деталей, окрашенных масляной краской, делали строения нарядными и праздничными. Даже сегодня, когда дома имеют далеко не первозданный вид, они продолжают радовать глаз, греют душу, поражают многообразием и неповторимостью деталей, фантазией и мастерством их творцов.

С целью сохранения культурно-исторического наследия в разные годы в Томске были созданы специализированная научно-производственная мастерская „Томскреставрация" (директор П.С. Сухотеплый) и сибирский филиал института „Спецпроектреставрация" (директор А.Н. Чернов). Институт выпускает научно-проектную документацию по реставрации и приспособлению памятников истории и архитектуры.

Для исторической части города разработаны проект охранных зон (ин-т „Спецпроектреставрация" г. Москва) и проект реконструкции центральной части (сибирский филиал ин-та „Спецпроектреставрация").

Учитывая богатое культурное наследие, Томску в 1990 году присвоен статус „исторического города". Для координации и решения проблем, связанных с сохранением этого наследия, в 1992 году создано муниципальное предприятие „Томск исторический".

В настоящее время состоят на государственной охране и имеют статус памятника 1697 объектов (в том числе памятники археологии). Среди памятников архитектуры большинство деревянных зданий. Большую тревогу вызывает то, что из-за недостатка финансов большинство готовой проектной документации по реставрации памятников не реализовано. В результате проекты морально устаревают, здания приходят в аварийное состояние, некоторые из них исчезают.

К отреставрированным объектам относятся памятники деревянного зодчества по ул. Красноармейская, 68 и проспекту Кирова, 7 (дом А.Д. Крячкова). Мне посчастливилось быть автором проектов реставрации этих замечательных представителей томского деревянного „модерна" и осуществлять авторский надзор.

2-х этажный деревянный дом по ул. Красноармейской, 68 (бывш. Солдатской) был построен в начале 20 века по проекту К.К. Лыгина в качестве жилого дома. Большой ущерб памятнику был нанесён пожаром 1977 г.

Уникальное для Томска, здание несёт в себе черты скандинавской архитектуры и отличается высоким качеством строительных работ.

Декоративные элементы „дракона", детали фронтонов воссозданы заново по шаблонам. Шаблоны выполнялись по сохранившимся остаткам деталей и фото до реставрации. Козырёк главного входа воссоздан по эскизу на основании обмеров сохранившихся врубок, рисунков К. К. Лыгина, найденных в архиве и аналогичного декора на башенках здания. Цветовое решение предложено на основании колера, найденного в главице „дракона." Инженером Резниковым А. В. был выполнен проект приспособления под поликлинику, которая разместилась в памятнике после реставрации. Реставрационные работы выполнены СНРПМ „Томскреставрация" в 1978-1982 гг.

Бывший особняк гражданского инженера А. Д. Крячкова построен в 1910 году по проекту А. Д. Крячкова. Проектом предусматривалась реставрация фасадов в первоначальном виде на основании архивных фотоматериалов, натурных исследований и проекта А. Д. Крячкова. После пожара 1982 года проектные работы выполнялись архитектором Ю. И. Бардочевым и конструктором С. Ф. Шатовым. Реставрация выполнена СНРПМ „Томскреставрация" в 1981-1985 гг. В настоящее время в памятнике размещается учреждение.

Архитектор /подпись/ /Л. С. Романова/

Postscript

A number of persons gave me support and assistance on my two visits to Siberia: Foremost among them were Dr. Paul Gutzwiller, who cooperated with the Institute of Archaeology and Ethnography of the Russian Academy of Science in Novosibirsk, his collaborator Anna Lutsidarskaya, the interpreter Irina Beresina, and Valeri Sherbakov.

In Tomsk I was assisted by the chairman of the town council, Anatoli Cherkassky, and Georg Shakhtarin, a member of the cultural council. I should like to express my special thanks to them all. This book project met with a particularly sympathetic response from the architect Larisa S. Romanova, head of the technical department of the Institute "Spezproiektrestravratsia", who herself has written a contribution.

Finally I should like to thank Roland Schweitzer for having written the preface and the team at Birkhäuser Publishers and Charles von Büren for their efforts to ensure the high quality of this book, and also my friends and colleagues without whose generous financial support this publication would not have been possible:

Burckhardt & Partner, Basel
Bürgin Nissen Wentzlaff, Basel
Hans Diehl, Kirchberg
Ernst Koller, Binningen
Edouard Lüdi, Basel
Silvia und Alfredo Mariani, Bottmingen
Rudolf Meyer, Basel
Harry Morath, Basel
Klaus Schuldt, Basel
Wilfrid und Katharina Steib, Basel
Hans Zwimpfer, Basel

I should thus like to express my sincere gratitude to all who have assisted me, in the hope that this publication will contribute to an urgently needed dialogue between East and West. Not only do the industrious people of Siberia deserve sympathy and affection, but the people of Tomsk must also receive material support in saving these magnificent wooden houses from rapid decay.

Postface

Au cours des deux voyages que j'ai effectués en Sibérie, j'ai bénéficié de l'aide et de l'appui de plusieurs personnes, au premier rang desquelles Paul Gutzwiller, qui a collaboré avec l'Institut d'archéologie-ethnographie de l'Académie russe des sciences de Novossibirsk, ainsi que sa collaboratrice Anna Luzidarskaia, Irina Beresina, traductrice, et Valeri Cherbakov.

A Tomsk, c'est au président du Conseil de la Ville, Anatoli Tcherkasski, et à Georg Chachtarin, membre du Conseil de la culture, que s'adresse tout particulièrement ma reconnaissance. J'ai en outre trouvé auprès de Mme Larisa S. Romanova, architecte et directrice de la section technique de l'Institut Spezprojektrestawrazia (spécialisé dans les projets de restauration), auteur d'un chapitre de ce livre, compréhension et intérêt pour ma démarche.

Enfin, je tiens à remercier Roland Schweitzer, qui a écrit la préface de ce livre, ainsi que les Editions Birkhäuser et Charles von Büren, qui ont œuvré pour la grande qualité; à cette expression de ma gratitude j'associe aussi mes amis et collègues qui, par leur généreux appui financier à cet ouvrage, ont permis que sa publication ait lieu:

Burckhardt & Partner, Basel
Bürgin Nissen Wentzlaff, Basel
Hans Diehl, Kirchberg
Ernst Koller, Binningen
Edouard Lüdi, Basel
Silvia und Alfredo Mariani, Bottmingen
Rudolf Meyer, Basel
Harry Morath, Basel
Klaus Schuldt, Basel
Wilfrid und Katharina Steib, Basel
Hans Zwimpfer, Basel

Réitérant à tous l'expression de ma vive reconnaissance, j'espère que cet ouvrage contribuera à un dialogue Est-Ouest de toute urgence nécessaire. Si le peuple sibérien appelle notre sympathie et notre affection, les gens de Tomsk demandent aussi à être matériellement aidés dans leurs efforts pour sauver d'une ruine imminente leurs splendides maisons en bois.

Nachwort

Verschiedene Personen standen mir auf meinen zwei Reisen nach Sibirien zur Seite: Allen voran Dr. Paul Gutzwiller, der mit dem Archäologisch-Ethnographischen Institut der Russischen Akademie der Wissenschaften Novosibirsk zusammenarbeitete, deren Mitarbeiterin Anna Luzidarskaja, die Dolmetscherin Irina Beresina und Waleri Scherbakow.

In Tomsk waren es der Vorsitzende des Stadtrates, Anatoli Tscherkasski, und Georg Schachtarin, ein Mitglied des Kulturrates. Ihnen allen möchte ich meinen besonderen Dank aussprechen. Großes Verständnis für dieses Buchprojekt zeigte insbesondere die Architektin Larisa S. Romanova, die Leiterin der Technischen Abteilung des Instituts «Spezprojektrestawrazia», die ja selbst einen Beitrag für dieses Buch verfaßt hat.

Schließlich danke ich Roland Schweitzer für das Geleitwort sowie dem Birkhäuser Verlagsteam und Charles von Büren für die großen Bemühungen um die hohe Qualität dieses Buches, aber auch meinen Freunden und Kollegen, die durch ihre großzügige Unterstützung diese Publikation überhaupt erst ermöglicht haben:

Burckhardt & Partner, Basel
Bürgin Nissen Wentzlaff, Basel
Hans Diehl, Kirchberg
Ernst Koller, Binningen
Edouard Lüdi, Basel
Silvia und Alfredo Mariani, Bottmingen
Rudolf Meyer, Basel
Harry Morath, Basel
Klaus Schuldt, Basel
Wilfrid und Katharina Steib, Basel
Hans Zwimpfer, Basel

So danke ich allen aufrichtig und in der Hoffnung, daß diese Publikation zu einem dringend notwendigen Dialog zwischen Ost und West beiträgt. Dem rührigen sibirischen Volk gebührt Sympathie und Liebe, die Menschen in Tomsk müssen aber auch materiell bei ihrem Bemühen unterstützt werden, diese prachtvollen Holzhäuser vor dem baldigen Zerfall zu retten.

Basel, im November 1993 — Werner Blaser

The town of Tomsk in the
17th century.

Tomsk au XVIIe siècle.

Die Stadt Tomsk
im 17. Jahrhundert.

A further lesson for construction with wood today

Mies van der Rohe, Japan, Gerrit Thomas Rietveld, the Hochschule für Gestaltung in Ulm and Alvar Aalto – these were five key, formative influences on Werner Blaser's development as architect and designer. As section headings in this book, each serves as a thematic point of reference through which to examine Werner Blaser's thought and work as a designer tody and, specifically, his concern with structure and design of furniture making – with strut and plane, with joint and connection.

Werner Blaser
**Joint and Connection /
Fügen und Verbinden**
Furniture design and their background /
Möbelentwicklungen und ihre Voraussetzungen

180 pages, 369 b/w ill.
22,5 x 23,5 cm. Hardcover.
ISBN 3-7643-2647-6
(English / German)

Une leçon exemplaire pour la construction en bois d'aujourd'hui

L'oeuvre de Werner Blaser, architecte, designer et homme de plume bâlois, porte l'empreinte des étapes qui ponctuent sa biographie professionelle: la rencontre avec Ludwig Mies van der Rohe, le Japon, Gerrit, Thomas Rietveld, la Hochschule für Gestaltung à Ulm, Alvar Aalto. Dans son travail s'exprime la volonté de réunir art du mobilier et art bâtir en un seul ouvrage, dont l'esthétique réside dans la structure renduc évidente. La création de meubles suit alors une espèce de systématique, qui cherche à épuiser les multiples possibilités de la construction géométrique.

Ein weiteres Lehrstück zum heutigen Bauen mit Holz

Das Werk des Basler Architekten, Designer und Publizisten Werner Blaser ist geprägt von den Stationen seiner beruflichen Biographie: die Begegnung mit Mies van der Rohe, Japan, Gerrit Thomas Rietveld, die Hochschule für Gestaltung in Ulm und Alvar Aalto.
Seinem Schaffen liegt die Intention zugrunde, Möbel- und Baukunst in einem Gesamtkunstwerk zusammenzubringen, dessen Ästhetik im Sichtbarmachen der Konstruktion liegt. So entsteht eine Art Systematik des Möbelbaus, die die vielfältigen Möglichkeiten der geometrischen Konstruktion auszuschöpfen sucht.

Birkhäuser